UNFAIR
ADVANTAGE

THE UNDERGROUND BLUEPRINT
TO CREATING A MASSIVE MOVEMENT BY TURNING YOUR KNOWLEDGE INTO INCOME!

KEVIN DAVID

First Edition 2019
ISBN: 978-1-949696-21-9 (Mobi)
ISBN: 978-1-949696-22-6 (Epub)
ISBN: 978-1-949696-23-3 (Paperback)
ISBN: 978-1-949696-24-0 (Hardcover)

Printed in the United States of America

Published by:

Lasting Press
615 NW 2nd Ave #915
Canby, OR 97013

Book Development, and Cover by: Rory Carruthers Marketing
www.RoryCarruthers.com

For more information about Kevin David, please visit: www.OfficialKevinDavid.com

*Dedicated to my beautiful mother Lauren and father David,
who gave me every advantage in life through their
never-ending support and encouragement.*

Contents

Preface ix

Introduction 1

Part 1 - Choosing Your Niche 11

   Chapter 1: The Knowledge Economy 13

   Chapter 2: Uncovering Your Diamond in the Rough:
                    Proven Profitable Courses 19

   Chapter 3: The ONE Universal Constant: Why Some
                    People Are Rich While Others Aren't 33

   Chapter 4: Sippin' on GIN and Juice: The Secret to
                    Becoming a Millionaire 45

   Chapter 5: Uncovering Your Perfect Niche 55

   Chapter 6: One Question to Rule Them All 63

   Chapter 7: Remastered Worldview: How Your Paradigms
                    Shape Your Life 71

Part 2 - Building Your Tribe 75

   Chapter 8: The Lone Wolf: Stop Following the Crowd 77

   Chapter 9: Creating Your Movement: The Three
                    Requirements 81

   Chapter 10: Becoming the Creator 87

   Chapter 11: The "Just Do It" Mentality: Break Things
                    Quickly 91

   Chapter 12: Shattering the Glass Ceiling: How to Find
                    Your First Customers 97

   Chapter 13: The Big Three 101

Chapter 14: Owning the Communication Platform:
  Your Facebook Group 105

Chapter 15: Drawing Them In: How to Get More Email
  Addresses 119

Chapter 16: Funnels Are the Future 123

Chapter 17: The Infinite Free Traffic Monster: YouTube ... 127

Chapter 18: Invincible Omnipotent Impact: Your
  Following 131

Part 3 - Validating Your Course Idea with Real-World Data. 139

Chapter 19: Validating Your Niche 141

Chapter 20: Seeking Your Question Pattern 145

Chapter 21: The Only Four Reasons People Buy Courses... 151

Chapter 22: Why You? The Genuinity Complex 155

Chapter 23: Establishing Proof of Concept 163

Chapter 24: You Da' Real MVP: Your Minimum
  Viable Offer 179

Chapter 25: How to be "Beta" Than Your Competition 183

Part 4 - Organizing, Pricing, and Building Your Course for
Explosive Growth 187

Chapter 26: The Power of Organization and Change 189

Chapter 27: From Skeleton to Flesh and Bones 195

Chapter 28: How to Create Success Stories 201

Chapter 29: No Excuses: How to 10x Your Productivity
  and Output 205

Chapter 30: A Picture Paints a Thousand Words, But a
  Video Makes Millionaires 209

Chapter 31: Becoming a Maestro of Pricing 213

Chapter 32: The Internal Battle: Your Lazy Mind Vs.
  Your Conscious Mind 221

Chapter 33: Change Your Habits, Change Your Life........... 227

Part 5 - Technological Evolution... 235
Chapter 34: Becoming the Master.................................... 237
Chapter 35: From Stranger to Buyer: The Art of the
Sales Funnel 245

Part 6 - Marketing Mastery.. 251
Chapter 36: The Art of Storytelling.................................... 253
Chapter 37: Specific, Sequential Steps................................ 259
Chapter 38: The Remix to Ignition: Steps to a Perfect
Launch 265

Conclusion 279
Bonus Chapter 283
About the Author 289

Preface

What is the secret rich people know that the rest of us don't? I remember being obsessed with this question growing up. If everyone is the same species (human), with the same amount of hours in the day, why do some people live in mansions and drive exotic cars, while others struggle and live paycheck to paycheck?

The world has changed. Just a few short years ago, the way people became "rich" was by owning the most stuff: the most cars, the most land, the most buildings. Getting "rich" took an entire lifetime, if not multiple lifetimes and generations, to accomplish.

But now the most valuable real estate company owns none of the real estate—AirBnB.

And the most valuable transportation company owns none of the cars—Uber.

So what has changed?

How are these companies creating empires in just a few years without owning anything at all?

The *world* has changed, and *Unfair Advantage* is a blueprint for how **you**, no matter your situation or industry, can take advantage of the biggest underground economic opportunity since the invention of the internet.

Imagine if you could go back in time and invest your life savings into Amazon stock at the beginning. I truly believe what is contained inside this book is the closest thing to being able to do that.

Unfair Advantage is not just a book; it is the summary of years of research, sacrifice, and extremely hard work so that you, the reader, can absorb all of my trials and tribulations, successes and failures in a fraction of the time, effort, and money. This book is quite literally a step-by-step blueprint laid out by someone who has tried close to every way known to man to make money from a laptop, and who went from being an unfulfilled, number crunching accountant to teaching over a million entrepreneurs how to be successful in just 18 short months.

Most people believe they don't have what it takes to live the life they want to live, a life filled with real freedom, freedom to do what you want when you want, to earn enough money to fly to Thailand on a whim, and to never be told what to do again, by anyone.

Unfair Advantage reveals the most valuable lessons, translated into chronological, actionable steps, that I've learned going from an anxious, depressed corporate drone trapped in a cubicle to creating my dream life in 1.5 years.

You are about to dive into the most comprehensive book on how to free yourself financially while building a massive and passionate following, all while accomplishing something most people can only dream of: changing the world.

#1 Success Strategy

Overwhelming evidence shows that the readers of *Unfair Advantage* who experience the most explosive success have one thing in common...

They read the entire book before implementing, focusing on truly understanding the content, rather than just memorizing it.

To get the most out of *Unfair Advantage*, read it from start to finish, take detailed notes while you read, translate the content to YOUR specific passion and experience, and then reread the book and reference your notes wherever you need additional clarity—this time implementing the concepts as you go.

The hardest part about creating a million dollar business has nothing to do with business at all. It has to do with mastering your mind, mastering human nature, and mastering your habits. These small mental commitments and accountability strategies, when compounded, make a profound impact, so don't underestimate their value.

A Proven Process

Unfair Advantage is the culmination of YEARS of my life, tens of thousands of collective hours studying world-leading experts in marketing, buyer psychology, presentations, sales, copywriting, influence, and millions of dollars (of my own money) testing which strategies work and which don't. The process I share has been substantiated by my students' results; some of whom I'm proud to say are now millionaires and multi-millionaires.

Unfair Advantage is robust, and its structure has been designed specifically to bring you results. If you're looking for a get rich quick scheme, I suggest you face the reality that getting rich takes SMART work (NOT hard work), and you shouldn't be afraid of it.

There's a very important distinction between hard work and smart work. Countless people work extremely hard in office jobs in their cubicles or at McDonalds, working double shifts to make ends meet, and never achieve their dreams and goals because they *don't* have an *Unfair Advantage*. They are working hard, but they are NOT working smart.

You're reading this because you want real change.

You don't just want incremental improvements, you want massive, earth-shattering transcension into a new dimension of success. This book teaches you the fundamentals of business and mindset required for any level of success, and then lays out a step-by-step, practical blueprint applicable to the CURRENT WORLD.

So many books nowadays are completely irrelevant due to technological advancements. This book acknowledges the changing landscape of the digital age and provides a practical step-by-step blueprint anyone, anywhere, with enough smart work, can follow to create their dream life.

Mindset Matters

I used to think all mindset evolution was fluff and that skipping straight to the tactics was the fast track to success. What I realized, though, is that most people need the mindset far more than they need the tactics—which is why I focus on ONLY the critical elements of your own mind you must master to create your dream life and leave out any and all fluff—trust me when I say *this* is the stuff that counts. If you skip the mindset portions or any part of this book, you'll skip other things in life—because how you do one thing is how you do everything.

No matter how beautiful your car looks, it won't go very far without the engine powering it, and without the engine, which is your mindset, you can never reach your true potential.

People ask me every day, "Kevin, what is the difference between your millionaire students and those who never achieve that level of success if they're both taking the same training?"

My answer is always one word, "Mindset."

Mindset affects everything—from the business and investment

decisions you make to your stress levels and overall happiness and fulfillment. Life isn't about how you perform when things are going well. It's more about how you perform when things are bad. It's important to learn how to protect your downside. When things go wrong, which they will, how can you pull through unfazed?

The decision to understand myself and my own mindset was the best decision and investment I've ever made. This was where all of the positive change really started to happen in my life.

Anyone can watch a motivational YouTube video, feel good, and hustle hard for a day or a week, but what often happens is that people drift back into their normal routine, only to feel as though they've made no progress at all.

The difference between those people and the people who succeed is mindset, worldview, and paradigm, which we will discuss later on.

This isn't some magical loophole which enables you to exploit some "rare" opportunity for a short amount of time. This isn't a hack to start making money overnight. This is about real, long-term, massive, meaningful improvement and mastery.

The most important thing I can possibly tell you is: **do the work.** If you show up, take notes, get motivated temporarily, but don't do the work, I can guarantee nothing is going to improve for you. You must learn, keep an open mind, and most importantly **take action.** Don't allow yourself to fall into the infinite learning cycle where so many entrepreneurs find themselves—where they feel as though they're making progress because they're learning and learning and learning, but never have any time to implement what they've learned! You must commit to reading this book. Wherever you are in the world right now, you can see the ink in the letters on this page— make an oath to me and to yourself, that this is the last time—block out all the noise, trust the results. It's not just me—look at Tony Robbins, Russell Brunson, Grant Cardone, all of these incredible entrepreneurs. What do they sell?

Information. Knowledge. Digital Courses.

This book is for long-sighted empire builders, the people who are willing to do what it takes to get what they want. They understand life isn't fair and want to learn the best way to harness the truest *Unfair Advantage* in business while helping others and finding fulfillment.

Follow the proven blueprint and seek to understand. Don't merely absorb the facts at face value. Instead, take a step back and examine the structure of the knowledge. Ask yourself what's working and why. Consider why I do what I do to be successful. This is how you convert knowledge into understanding, and it's what you'll need to do to take full advantage of this book and transform your life.

Introduction

L ess than two years ago, I had zero followers and had never even heard of digital marketing. Since then, I've built a $10MM+ business that operates on autopilot and, more importantly, have helped over a million people on their path to financial freedom—but it wasn't always this way.

My path was far from unique, and was even further from a fairytale. I went to college, like most people, and like most, I didn't know what to study. I had no idea how the "real world" worked. But everything happened exactly as it was meant to, just like everything in your life up until this moment has happened as it was meant to.

I've always been a fan of getting to the point, but a bit of backstory is necessary to illustrate how I stumbled upon the greatest business opportunity on Earth and how I discovered the underground movement that is the *Unfair Advantage*.

Growing up, I lived a relatively normal life with amazing, supportive parents with very traditional mentalities when it came to finances and business. They always told me to go to school, get a job, and save for retirement—and as most children do, I listened to them, went to high school, got reasonable grades without much interest or work, and then attended college.

After graduating *summa cum laude* from Oregon State Honors College, I pursued a career as an accountant (because my parents and guidance counselors told me to major in something I could actually find a job in) for PricewaterhouseCoopers in Portland, Oregon.

There were nearly five hundred applicants for this so-called "coveted" consulting position. Everyone around me convinced me to feel proud and grateful to be the one selected when so many others were not.

It really felt like I was on the right track. I was doing everything right by graduating with honors and being hired for a coveted position by a successful, multinational company. Everything was going amazing from an outside perspective.

The problem was, it didn't feel amazing; it felt tedious, devoid of passion, boring, and unfulfilling. I did not feel happy or fulfilled and struggled to find balance and meaning in my life. I quickly realized that working eighty-hour weeks making someone else rich was not the life for me.

So, I transitioned and began working as a privacy consultant at Facebook in Menlo Park, California. They are known for having some of the most generous employee perks in the world, including on-site doctors, free food, ice cream parlors, and oil changes in the parking lot. I felt like this had to be where I belonged!

It had to be...

Facebook was one of the most prestigious places to work in the world. Everyone dreams of working at Facebook. Again, it was amazing from the outside looking in.

But the problem was, it still wasn't right for me. I started to wonder if there was something wrong with me. How could I still be unhappy working at one of the most prestigious companies in the world?

Up until that point, I never really understood what an entrepreneur was. I had heard the word and knew of the legends of entrepreneurship, but I didn't really understand what it meant at its core. It wasn't until I discovered that core understanding that I started down my true path.

My True Path

I knew I had to make a change and find my true path in life. I wanted to figure out how I could free myself to travel the world and live life on my own terms while also finding fulfillment in my work. I remember speaking to HR at my 9-5 company as they proudly shared that they offered two weeks of vacation per year.

I remember asking about the other 50 weeks…

I naturally questioned the "status quo" the way entrepreneurs do, without even realizing it.

It was at that point I really started to meaningfully explore online sources of income. I didn't have some epic tale or lightbulb moment. Entrepreneurship isn't like a movie; there isn't some beautiful, simple moment where you achieve perfect clarity. There is never a perfect time to start, and I don't have some interesting story—I literally started out by Google searching "How to make money online."

However, after doing a ton of research, I started to implement what I learned. I wrote a travel blog, I created a mobile iOS app, I tried affiliate marketing on Amazon, but none of those brought the life-changing success I was looking for. Naturally, I began to question myself again. Did I make a mistake? Am I not smart enough? I started to question everything—were my parents, my friends, my family, and my co-workers right? Was I crazy for wanting more?

Luckily, I had enough belief in myself and my abilities to understand this was simply self-doubt creeping in to challenge my resolve.

Because I knew self-doubt was coming, I was ready. I never even considered going back to my 9-5. I was so far removed from that even being an option that I would have slept on the floor before I gave up and crawled back to my dress shirt and cubicle.

Right about that time, I stumbled upon Amazon FBA (again from a Google search) as a source of revenue through their Fulfillment by Amazon (FBA) program. Everyone I knew was shopping on Amazon (myself included), and I could sense that society was moving toward using Amazon more and more for everyday purchases.

I again jumped in headfirst, after doing my due diligence, and ended up purchasing six different products to sell on Amazon in my first order. I consolidated them all into one shipping container (to save money as my budget was very limited) and financed them primarily through a 0% APR credit card.

Within the first week of my products being live on Amazon, I was making more than I was at my 9-5 job, and I was making it from my laptop, from home.

I started to look for ways to learn more and stumbled across what, at the time, was the largest Facebook group in the world for Amazon sellers, which had over 29,000 people in it.

I remember being blown away. I reached out to the admin of the group, who happened to be from a small town near where I grew up in Oregon, and I asked him how on earth he gathered all those people in one place!

He told me most of his group came from his YouTube channel. It was at that moment I had the first and probably only true epiphany I've had in my entrepreneurial career.

It's a beautiful thing when the dots finally connect. Although entrepreneurship is not like a movie, this was the closest thing I've ever experienced to it, when the light bulb turned on.

My passion in life has always been teaching. I used to tutor people in calculus and accounting for free, just because I enjoy seeing the lightbulb turn on as people connect the dots. But I also enjoy financial freedom, and unfortunately, being a traditional teacher and financial freedom don't usually align due to salary restrictions. I realized I could teach people on YouTube and hoped I could eventually monetize it in a way that allowed me the level of financial freedom I wanted.

When I was first starting on YouTube, I had no idea what I was doing. I was recording my videos from my phone and laptop camera with no mic and no lighting. I was just creating because it was fun! I remember people telling me, "Kevin, don't start YouTube, it's saturated, it's too late," which is the same thing people told me when I was starting Amazon. I started to notice a pattern: most people give really bad advice when it comes to entrepreneurship. You should only listen to a few select people who've proven they know what they're talking about—and thoroughly and completely ignore everyone else.

YouTube was no fairy tale either. I created videos that took me hours or days to complete and barely anyone watched them. However, like most "overnight successes," after a lot of smart work and dedication…

BOOM! All of a sudden, one of my videos about Amazon went viral while I was at Carnival in Brazil. From that point until the time writing this, I've gained over 600,000 subscribers on YouTube and a following of well over 1,000,000 entrepreneurs!

I realized all the incremental efforts and compound interest of my actions were starting to come back to me. All of a sudden, my videos were getting a ton of views and people were asking how they could get my "course." At the time, I didn't even know what a course was. I remember having to Google search "What is a course" to figure out how to go about creating one.

I knew that any type of one-on-one consulting wasn't what I wanted. It's hard work, time intensive, and manual—*not* smart work. There's no scale in something that directly requires your one-on-one attention.

Smart work was creating something I could sell that could help thousands of people automatically without any of my manual input.

So through the alignment of the universe and a lot of smart work, I came to the conclusion that I needed to be focusing all my time creating a digital course teaching others what I knew about Amazon. As a course creator, I could embrace my passion for teaching and have the ability to pursue real financial freedom while also working for myself and helping others find fulfillment.

It wasn't until I had created my digital course that I started to understand success is not linear, it's exponential. This was one of the most important realizations of my life.

Exponential Growth

Success exists on an exponential growth curve. We take incremental action by reaching out to one more lead or potential customer, calling one more prospect, making one more YouTube video, or doing one more hour of product research for our eCommerce store. It feels like we are doing all this work, but nothing is changing, so we give up.

Albert Einstein said that compound interest is the eighth wonder of the world. "He who understands it, earns it…he who doesn't…pays it."

Life as an entrepreneur is exactly the same. We take consistent, incremental actions every day, things that at the time feel small, like five more minutes research on Google or ten more minutes learning on YouTube. If you look at any one day, it feels like hardly any progress is being made—but compounded, these actions make ALL the difference.

People start a journey and don't see the rewards from their efforts immediately, so they give up and quit before the point at which their incremental daily effort begins compounding.

Time compounds incremental daily action exponentially.

Modern society has made entrepreneurship and starting your own business out to be some massive gamble where only 1% of people are lucky enough to be successful, and anyone, anywhere who makes a lot of money is fortunate, or it's a façade, and their Lamborghini must be leased and their mansion rented.

Most people think my success is because I'm privileged. They assume I am a trust fund baby. That's not true at all. People aren't successful due to luck. I don't believe there is such a thing as luck.

There is a dedicated focus on the RIGHT THING, the smart thing, and there is everything else. Luck is simply being focused on the right thing and being in "the race." Think about it like this: you can't win first place in a race if you don't even enter it. Luck is the same way, you have to be *in the right race* to have a chance at winning, and the only way you do that is by focusing on the right thing.

Cause and Effect

When I made the decision to quit my job as an accountant, I doubted myself. I worried I was making the wrong decision. All of my co-workers and friends and family thought I was crazy. I had already invested all that time at college, and now I wasn't even going to use it.

If we were to look at its resounding effect of that one seemingly insignificant decision, we would see it has generated more than $10,000,000 in less than 18 months, from nothing. That's massive! But if you asked me the day I quit, I would have told you I was nervous, I was worried, it didn't feel right, and everyone around me, including my family, friends, and co-workers thought I was crazy.

You have something invaluable I didn't have, which is HARD EVIDENCE that this works. I had nothing but blind faith in myself and a burning desire for something more.

Everything in this life is cause and effect, and it's compounded exponentially over time. When you're taking action every day, when you choose to put an hour into your business today, or when you decide to make a post in your Facebook group or create a YouTube video, you have to consider its effect in the long term.

If you just make one small move today, I can't tell you how life-changing it will be. The impact of it on your future is greater than you can possibly imagine. Rome wasn't built in a day, and neither is your movement. It will be the compounding exponential effect of daily effort no matter how small.

Believe in Yourself

If you believe you'll be successful and work hard, you will be successful. If you're planning for anything else, you won't be successful.

I was the person who used to think, "Ugh, mindset stuff…Can we get to the tactics?" When I had that thought pattern, I didn't achieve anything. That is when I began to study myself, my choices, and the outcomes those choices brought about.

I've observed with meticulous detail, not just with myself, but over 10,000 students who've come through all of my programs. The people who get the best results, change their lives, and have massive transformations begin with their mindset.

I really encourage you to let go of any negative sentiments or feelings of uselessness or dread concerning learning about mindset. Often, someone will just work at the logical stuff. They'll get frustrated and burnt out, or they will lose focus and drift back to their comfort zone and the patterns their brain is used to.

I used to just teach tactics, but I noticed people didn't get the massive results I knew they should be getting. They understood the tactics, but because they didn't believe in themselves and didn't have good habits and motivation, they wouldn't implement them consistently.

Even if they understood the tactics, they didn't feel worthy of success or believe they were capable of breaking out of their comfort zone.

One of the most meaningful things I can possibly teach you is that whatever you *think* is what you end up thinking about, and then what you think about is what you think, and this is a never-ending cycle...

Before you say, "Wait what?" let me explain with a short story...

Growing up, one of my teachers said I was terrible at math, and because they said that to me, I believed it. It set off a spiral and formed what I like to call a "Thought Plague," which then formed a belief, which then became an ultimate reality. One tiny thought can set off a chain reaction and make somebody depressed and broken OR confident and unbreakable very quickly—depending on what thoughts are reinforced.

Let me illustrate how that chain reaction can occur: if I hadn't made that one tiny, seemingly insignificant decision to quit my job as an accountant and give entrepreneurship a try, you wouldn't be reading this, the thousands of people whose lives have completely changed because of my training might still be trapped in their 9-5 jobs, and I wouldn't have generated over ten million dollars in 18 months, because of ONE THOUGHT and ONE DECISION in ONE MOMENT.

You can use this in your life too; you can either have positive thought cycles or negative ones. What you think about is what you think about, and what you think about becomes what you believe, and what you believe becomes your reality. It is time to shift your mindset, learn some powerful strategies, and create the reality you've always dreamed of.

Let's do this together.

Part 1
Choosing Your Niche

Chapter 1
The Knowledge Economy

"I'm not a businessman, I'm a business, man!"
— Jay Z

Out with the Old, In with the New

Have you ever asked yourself, "What is a business, really?" The traditional answer most people would give is that a business has a storefront, an office building, a warehouse, sells physical products, inventory, and has a large staff sitting in cubicles.

This model works, but it's dated. It is expensive, time-consuming, and not infinitely scalable. It also comes with much more risk than the new and improved model. The old model used to be the only real way to create a multi-million dollar business. It took years, a ridiculous amount of work, employees, office space, and expenses to do it. *Not anymore.*

If you're reading this, you're officially out of the minor leagues. This is no longer about scraping by or just making enough to live. This is for people who want to make life-changing money, and more importantly, create a global movement and help countless people while doing it. There is nothing like getting messages from students saying you changed their lives and their families' lives. It is seriously powerful stuff.

Turn What You Know into Dough

The new model is what economists call the **Knowledge Economy**, which means every single person has a business inside of them, by virtue of their own unique past experiences and personal knowledge.

Let's say you make the *best* blueberry muffins in the entire world. Using the old business model, you might decide to open a bakery. You'd be forced to undergo all the trials and tribulations of launching a brick and mortar business (cost of goods sold, employees, rent, insurance, office space, etc.).

What if, instead, you leverage the internet to teach people how to bake the perfect blueberry muffins themselves? This business plan involves less hassle, fewer startup costs, and less work. Instead of just reaching a few thousand customers in your area, you could potentially market your product to millions of people around the world.

The new model not only leverages you, but it leverages technology to boost you into an omnipresent machine, impacting more people than you ever thought possible in your wildest dreams. Instead of helping people one-on-one, you're helping hundreds or thousands of people with no additional manual time or effort on your part.

A video can play again and again and again to millions of people with no additional effort on your behalf; it just keeps going. It's like hiring an infinite, never-tiring workforce. By replacing your teaching effort with the inner workings of the automated machine, you become a superhero by simulating the one-on-one or done-for-you client experience online in the form of your digital course movement.

Annihilating Trends and Seasonality

When I was first starting as an entrepreneur, I took all the money I had and invested in all types of businesses I thought people wanted. One of those businesses was an iOS app I created called QuizPixel. I was sure I was going to become the next app millionaire. I dedicated my life to it, every waking hour, second, and day to it, and I invested all the money I had plus more into this business. After months of twelve hour days and my entire life savings, plus debt pumped into it, I was finally ready to go to the market and start selling it.

No one bought it.

I'd built something nobody needed.

It taught me a lesson I'll never forget: you can try to be the next Elon Musk, create the next innovative start up, and be one in a billion, or you can do what works, but do it in a more efficient, intelligent, and scalable way. That led me to research what always "works" when it comes to the knowledge economy. I realized every multi-million dollar course can be boiled down to three overarching "evergreen" categories which the majority of people care about.

Evergreen Courses

There are three overarching categories all human beings care about deeply: health, wealth, and relationships. These categories will always be profitable!

The first three steps to creating a wildly successful online course:

1. Choose Your Evergreen Niche
2. Subclassification
3. Sub-Niche

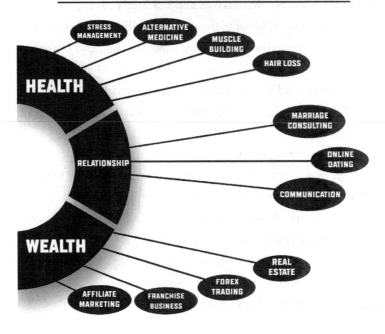

Narrowing Down Your Focus

Your topic is crucially important because it's really what you're selling to people. When you target everyone, you get no one. Imagine you're at a crowded airport and you shout, "Hey everyone!" No one is going to look. They're going to keep walking. However, if you ask "Hey, is anyone a doctor here?", the doctors are going to respond.

The same is true in the business world. Niche down, get specific, and become a true master. If you're not yet, that is okay. Everyone starts at the same position, but the interesting thing is you get good at what you do.

The riches are in the niches.

You don't have to be an expert to create a great product that helps people—you just have to be a few steps ahead of the beginners. You don't have to be the world's foremost expert on a subject to make a course, you just need to know more than those you teach, so the knowledge you teach your students is worth more than the money they pay you!

Chapter 2

Uncovering Your Diamond in the Rough: Proven Profitable Courses

"Information products are low-cost, fast to manufacture, and time-consuming for competitors to duplicate."
— Tim Ferriss

Timing can be everything in life. Many entrepreneurs have proven that no matter how good your product is, if you don't properly time the market, you're doomed.

While evergreen courses put you in the right playing field, you still want to give it a logic test and use good old fashioned data to help make your final decision.

Find the category and subclassification you're passionate about from the evergreen courses diagram in the previous chapter. Even if it is a topic others have covered previously, realize that the way you teach someone how to do something has its own unique intrinsic value. Here are some examples of how you can take your prior knowledge and experience and turn it into an evergreen course:

- How to use a software you already use (that makes people *money*)

- How to do a task you know how to do (that makes people *healthier*)

- How to use a platform or technology you use every day (that makes people *money*)

- How to strengthen relationships with loved ones in a way you feel comfortable with (that makes **relationships** stronger)

Competition Is a Good Thing

The best and easiest way to pick an idea for a course is to look at what other successful experts have done in the past and proven to be successful. A common *devastating* mistake beginners make is deciding to make a course on a topic no one else has ever made a course on before. This couldn't be further from the reality of how successful courses are made.

The goal is to make your proven course idea *better* than your competition. Understand that competition is often a good thing! Be more passionate and energetic! Caring more than anyone else and helping your students more one-on-one than anyone else in the niche is the proven way to be wildly profitable and impactful. You win by adding more value for free. Provide more guidance to your students and followers, and you will be successful!

These are a few examples of successful niches. Look specifically for prior winners in a similar niche to the one you wish to enter.

EXAMPLES OF PROVEN COURSE TOPICS:
How to Lose Post-Pregnancy Baby Fat
How to Meditate

How to Paint

How to Garden

How to Quit Watching Porn

How to Run Facebook Ads

How to Run an Airbnb

How to Be a Landlord

How to Fly a Drone

How to Make a Profitable Accounting Business

How to Have a Better Memory

How to Do Small Business Taxes

Never force your course topic. Evaluate the data, the market, and what is already working, and create the *next* best course. Be objective; falling in love with your course topic without data backing it is the surest way to failure.

Some students have had massive success in learning new pieces of software that support small businesses and making tutorials on them. I usually Google search "best new software for small businesses" and look for the newest articles to see if people are talking about them or using them. If it's brand new software, no one is an expert, so you can forge the first path and become the go-to person for that software. If it makes people money, and you're the best at it, it will make you money!

Don't think you're marrying your choice of niche/topic for the rest of your life. The decision you make is by no means final. If you pick Amazon, you're not stuck with Amazon.

Don't fall victim to decision paralysis—not being able to decide and being torn between multiple things. You can come up with four or five ideas for a niche, and then pick one from those five. There is absolutely no reason why you can't choose one. It doesn't matter if you get it wrong, you can always change it later, but you need to pick something to start.

I encourage you to pick your own niche; however, I'm also going to teach you some things about digital marketing in this book. There is virtually an infinite number of businesses that could benefit from digital marketing, so if you can't think of anything, you can use this as a last resort plan to just get started.

You can become an expert at digital marketing for plastic surgeons, insurance agents, plumbers, or any number of businesses—remember the riches are in the niches. You always make more at being the best at a specific thing than a generalist at everything. Remember, you get good at what you do. If you are good at getting new paying customers with digital marketing for a specific type of cash-rich businesses, you'll be just fine.

People make many thousands of dollars teaching accountants how to build profitable practices, or run ads for plumbers, or SEO for dentists because there are thousands of these businesses that all need help finding new profitable customers. If you become a known expert, it's a quick way to make a lot of money and help a lot of people. I know it might sound crazy now, but there are millions to be made with digital marketing for cash-rich businesses, and when you become the best at Facebook Ads for Dentists or Google Ads for Real Estate agents, the sky's the limit!

Inspiration

Don't worry about taking inspiration from other people's course landing pages, descriptions, webinars, and public information. Obviously, don't copy anything, but it is not immoral to take inspiration from other successful people; you're a fool if you don't. You can develop your own understanding of the subject much further by studying the incumbents and pre-existing successful people and learning from them. It expedites your learning curve immeasurably by doing so.

Think about it like this: do new books from *other* authors help or hurt an established author? The answer to this is known as the car dealership effect: whether your competitors do a lousy job or a great job, they HELP you because if they do a great job, they bring more people into the niche, and if they do a terrible job, it makes your product look amazing by comparison!

By doing great, you can manage to get sales and take advantage of your competitors. You can win no matter what if you perform better; that is the beauty of a capitalistic society. Be creative and ethical, and you'll be fine. As long as there is a problem in your niche, there is room for an opportunity to become better and create new ideas.

Pain and Pleasure

Why are some courses wildly successful while others flounder?

People buy when they're in pain and in need of a solution to a problem. The ONLY two reasons people buy anything is to move away from pain or toward pleasure. It's one of the intrinsic desires all humans share, and it needs to be the foundation of your course topic.

Why is Uber so successful? Anyone who has taken a lot of taxis knows why. Getting a taxi is a major pain! Most of the drivers are rude and overcharge you, and finding one when you need one can be awful.

The Pain

All great products focus on pain—not just online courses—all great products, period.

The best courses solve a specific pain, just like Uber does. For example, one of the best-selling online dating products was a product called Double Your Dating by David DeAngelo. He released it years ago, and it's still around today. The pain it solves? Guys getting rejected by beautiful women and feeling the pain of rejection. He helps them get dates and solves that pain.

Another example is Mike Geary's *Truth About Abs*. He built a simple product about abs into a business that has generated more than $1,000,000 per month. How? People wanted abs, tried everything to get them, and failed. They felt the pain of not being in shape or not getting attention from the opposite sex, and his course relieved that pain.

The Pleasure

Once you find the pain, the next step is just as simple. The difference? Before you were looking for pain, now you're looking for pleasure. Again, people only do things to either:

a.) Alleviate pain

b.) Pursue pleasure

Once you know the pain and the pleasure, your online course should be a course that walks people through how to go from pain to pleasure.

Examples of Pain + Pleasure:

Pain #1: "I was treated poorly by a man whom I thought cared about me, but he left me when something more interesting came up..."
Pleasure #1: Never Be Second Choice Again: How to Make a Man Treat You like a Goddess!

Pain #2: "I wish I would have known how to be a respected member of my relationship. I did everything wrong! He must think I'm a total wimp, and he's now got an even bigger ego."

Pleasure #2: Stand Up for Yourself: How to Win Respect from Your Partner!

Pain #3: "My relationship unexpectedly fell apart completely, and now I'm alone and lonely."
Pleasure #3: How to Get Past a Broken Relationship and Find Your Soulmate!

Every single human being on Earth instinctually wants to move **away** from pain and **toward** pleasure, but to get to pleasure, your future students need to overcome a series of **obstacles**.

It's your job to anticipate those obstacles. Eventually, it's your job to help your students get past those obstacles or remove them completely.

Let's say you're creating a course on getting a job as a computer programmer. What could the transformation look like?

Pain: No one wants to hire me

Obstacle #1: How do I update my resume to draw attention?

Obstacle #2: How do I find internship opportunities?

Obstacle #3: How do I create an online portfolio?

Obstacle #4: How do I improve my interviewing skills?

Obstacle #5: Where can I find networking events in my area?

Pleasure: I got hired as a computer programmer!

The Struggle

So how do you figure out what people's pain is when it comes to your niche? Ask some form of the "What are you struggling with?" question.

It could be:

- "What are you struggling with when it comes to…?"
- "What's your biggest challenge?"
- "What's holding you back?"
- "How does it make you feel when you try to do X?"

If you're not sure where to find people to ask and you don't have a following yet, join a few relevant Facebook groups and interact with the members.

What's a relevant group? Well, if you want to create a photography course for beginners, don't join a group of professional photographers. Look for people who are just getting started. Type Photography into the Facebook search bar and filter to see groups.

Don't just spam people in the group. Read the questions people are asking. What problems do they have? What are their sticking points? Which questions come up again and again? Contribute and be helpful. Then ask, "What are you struggling with?"

Do not just rely on friends and family. You can use real market data to see the real questions and concerns people have related to your niche!

You can find popular books on almost any niche. Read reviews or conversations on these topics to see why real people in the market are in pain and how this strategy brought them pleasure. Then reverse engineer the exact pain point "words" they use to understand their pleasure and focus on how your course could get them from their pain to their desired result—pleasure.

Look for commonalities and patterns in people's questions. Think about what's really going on. Instead of imagining problems people might have, go out into the market and do some remarkable market research.

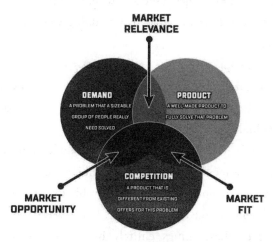

PRODUCT MARKET FIT

"PRODUCT/MARKET FIT MEANS BEING IN A GOOD MARKET
WITH A PRODUCT THAT CAN SATISFY THAT MARKET."
— MARC ANDREESSEN

The Art of Picking a Niche

You need to have a large enough audience that you can target and sell courses to, but a specific enough audience to be able to target accurately.

BAD EXAMPLE: Fitness

GOOD EXAMPLE: Fitness Workout Plan for New Mothers to Help Lose Their Baby Weight

Never Reinvent the Wheel

Once you've decided on a niche, deeply research what others have done in the same or similar niche. Remember, you always want to use what is actually proven.

Let's say you find a sub-niche you're interested in. Now, your sole mission is to find every single successful person and absolutely devour their websites, sales pages, social media presence, YouTube, Instagram, etc. and look for what they're doing well and what you can **improve**.

Hunt these people down like you're a lion starving for food, and they're the last gazelle on the savannah. Subscribe to their email lists, take notes, eat, sleep, and breathe what they have done, and continuously look for ways to improve on it!

You will want to recreate what they have done, add your own twist, and do it better. People have spent millions on copywriters to write their emails, people to design their webinars, people to make their ads, and you can see this all for free. Don't waste money—you can do most of these things entirely by yourself at first, then outsource when it is smart to do so.

A New Opportunity

To make a home-run course, you need to frame your offer as a new opportunity, not an improvement.

Think about the Keto diet as an example. It was not just another diet everyone had tried. It was not just sticking to the same boring foods. This was science; this was brand new; this was what everyone was talking about, and it was a revolutionary way to get healthier.

When you try to sell something people have already tried and failed, you can never sell it to them. When you sell something brand new and sexy that people have never previously failed at, you may strike gold!

This may not seem like a significant difference, but it is mentally. People dread things they already know are hard, and are excited for new opportunities to get their desired results *without* the pain associated with hard work!

Your new fitness program is not an improvement on an existing plan but a brand new, never done before, revolutionary program.

It is much more difficult to **improve** because in people's minds, improvement is associated with something difficult. People tend to attach negative thoughts with "improving." New opportunities present an opening for people to change their lives!

The "Big Money" is always in teaching beginners. I know it may seem tempting to create an intermediate to advanced level course, but generally, when people reach that level of expertise, they don't look for courses, as they are more comfortable teaching themselves at that stage. Teaching a course centered around beginners is always going to be more profitable and impactful in the end!

You want to always ask yourself: is my course going to take a beginner with no pre-existing skills and teach them how to make $3-5k per month, or lose 15 pounds in 90 days, or have confidence talking to women?

What's in a Name? - Your Catchphrase

When you create your course, it is critical to understand your catchphrase. All successful courses have them, and in the simplest sense, your catchphrase describes what desire your course will provide to your end customer in one sentence or less!

> *Catchphrase Examples:*
> *How to Buy Real Estate With Little or No Money Down*
> *How to Lose Weight After a New Baby Without Giving Up the Foods You Love*
> *How to Create a Fully Scalable Online Business Without Any Previous Experience or Technical Skills*

This basically serves as a one-line descriptor of your course after the course name itself. It should provide a bit of additional detail.

> *Title:* *Digital Course Secrets*
> *Catchphrase:* *"How to Create a Hyper Profitable Digital Course Without ANY Experience, Technical Skill, or Pre-Existing Expertise"*

Your Brand Name

I recommend creating a personal brand, meaning your name, or something close to your name. If you have a difficult to pronounce first or last name, I recommend simplifying them or even creating an online pseudonym.

This is more common than you might think—just ask Eldrick "Tiger" Woods :)

Names that are easy to pronounce and two syllables or less always tend to do better and are more easily memorable. If 'Hardunkachud' was my actual last name, but no one could pronounce or remember it, I would simply change it to be something more memorable.

I chose Kevin David because I wanted to protect my parents' privacy, and I'm thankful I did! David vs. Goliath is a story I've always loved, and David is also my middle name, so I created my online persona or pseudonym as Kevin David.

Another example is my original branding, which was THATLifestyleNinja—general enough not to be pigeonholed into Amazon alone (which was my first course), but specific enough to signify a movement: becoming a Ninja and achieving the lifestyle you want.

I would strongly recommend using your name or pseudonym because you will get bored with a brand name eventually (as I did with THATLifestyleNinja), but your name is something you have forever. I ended up having to change all my branding from THATLifestyleNinja to Kevin David. It was a lot of work and confusion. Don't repeat the same mistake. Go with your personal brand with a simplified last name if you have a difficult one to pronounce and remember—such as "Kevin David."

Whatever you choose for your name or brand you're building, you want to ideally have the URL available, Facebook page name available, YouTube, Instagram, etc. Do not kill yourself here. If only some of the socials are available, proceed anyway. My social media is NOT exactly matching; I wish it were, but it didn't do too much harm.

If your personal brand name is not available as a URL, simply add "official" or "real" before or after; for example, my website is www.officialkevindavid.com!

- **Personal Brand** - Kevin David

- **Name for Audience** - Ninjas! (Other examples include Heroes, CEOs, Freedom Fighters, and Superstars)

"What is UP, NINJAS!" was the tagline I used to open every one of my YouTube videos, and people want to become Ninjas and join the Ninja family!

They also importantly refer to themselves as Ninjas, which gives brand identity and starts to build your CULT-ure. If you can build a cult-like following, making money in your life will be a piece of cake!

Chapter 3

The ONE Universal Constant: Why Some People Are Rich While Others Aren't

"Great works are performed, not by strength, but by perseverance."
— Samuel Johnson

Time is a universal constant. As humans, we all have the same amount of time and energy. We also have the free will to choose where to apply that time and energy.

Have you ever stopped to think that a billionaire and a homeless person are both, in essence, the same? The only difference is their experience, mentality, and directional focus. It is essential to realize what you spend energy on is going to detract that energy from something else. So, if you spend energy on social media or your image at first, it will detract from what you should be focusing on, which is finding your customers, establishing proof of concept, and creating a beautiful minimum viability product in the form of your course!

Expect Positive Outcomes

Near the beginning of the book, I briefly mentioned a teacher I had in elementary school who told me I was terrible at math. At the time, I believed it because I wasn't in a position to question the teacher. As a child, you are led to believe the teacher is right, and you are meant to follow their teachings.

Because of this, every time a math test came up, I said, "I can't do this." For my whole childhood, I dreaded math tests because I genuinely believed I wasn't good at math just because one teacher said it. I can't even remember her name at this point, but I will never forget what she said to me.

This is the power of a "Thought Plague" and the chain reaction that can ensue because of it. What one completely meaningless (in the grand scheme of my life) person said to me plagued my entire childhood, becoming self-fulfilling prophecy that I was awful at math. One meaningless comment, from one insignificant person, changed my entire perspective on my own abilities. She could have been going through a divorce, or her dog died the night before; it doesn't matter what was happening in her life when she said it. All that matters is that one insignificant comment multiplied and grew like a virus in my mind until it affected my entire worldview and perspective on my mathematical abilities.

Just as a teacher saying you're bad at math when you're a kid can make you horrible at math for life, you may believe you're bad at technology because someone told you so. It's a self-fulfilling prophecy. It's an evolution of a thought that has stemmed, become systemic, and taken over your mentality.

A compelling lesson I've learned is that all humans seek evidence to support what they believe and attempt to reject evidence that goes against it.

For example, if my teacher tells me I'm bad at math, my current situation says I'm bad at math. If there's a math test coming up, I think I'm doomed to fail, and if I think I'm going to fail, then my actions support that by not even trying to succeed through studying, because the evidence of my teacher saying I'm bad at math supports the outcome of me failing my math test.

Because I don't think I have a chance at succeeding, I don't study, and because I don't study, I fail, and because I fail, my initial belief that I never had a chance in the first place is confirmed. This realization was one of the most important in my life.

But what happens if you flip that same idea on its head?

If you set a positive outcome for the future, a funny thing happens. You take a ton of action, and when you do take a lot of action, you're exponentially more likely to experience a positive outcome that reinforces your initial positive outlook.

So if my teacher told me I was amazing at math, I would feel good hearing it, and that would become my belief. I would then study hard to ensure I maintained that high standard, and when I passed the test with flying colors, my belief would be confirmed, creating a positive feedback loop.

This is the visualization that actually works. Picture it enough times, ingrain it, etch it into your mind, and eventually, with enough consistent, focused action, it becomes a reality!

"Most of the important things in the world have been accomplished by people who have kept on trying when there seemed no hope at all."
— Dale Carnegie

People aren't dumb. The only reason people are dumb is because they think they're dumb. It's really as simple as that. This is coming from someone who thought he was dumb and who was told by teachers he was dumb.

No one is inherently dumb or bad at technology, some people just come more naturally into it because of their upbringing and experience with it. It's a mental block, nothing more.

To be successful, you need two things: belief and an unbreakable focus. You need to have the belief you can be successful because if you genuinely believe it, your actions will align with that belief, and with enough consistent effort, you will start to get results. When you get results, you will get confidence that feeds your belief, and the chain reaction becomes unstoppably positive.

Focus makes millionaires. Not only focusing on what you should do, but focusing on what you should not do, and then having the willpower to resist it.

Let's take a comparison between two people to illustrate:

Person A: Kevin—Works at McDonald's for 80 hours a week and makes $800 a week.

Person B: David - Works for himself starting a digital course.

After 90 days, Kevin has made $3,200 per month x 3 or $9,600 (I'm being generous here; obviously, there are taxes, etc.).

After 90 days, let's say David has made $0 for the sake of illustration, but has built 1,000 subscribers on YouTube and 500 members in his Facebook group, all of whom could become potential buyers for his course and all his future products, masterminds, events, etc. that he releases!

When he releases a product, let's say for $997, even at a 1% conversion rate, that is ten people from YouTube and five from Facebook, which is $15,000 (and 1% is a VERY conservative estimate).

Those people will buy from him again and again, and his following only compounds, grows, and builds exponentially while Kevin has nothing. If he left McDonald's, he would make $0 and probably have very little in savings.

Who would you rather be? I know this example is black and

white, but 99.9% of people on Earth choose person A, money now, instant gratification.

The easiest way I can cement this point is a cleaning business with one or two janitors. Let's say the maximum capacity of that janitor's business is thirty cleanings a month. If they were to scale that up to sixty cleanings, each job would get half the attention it usually would. If a janitor starts giving all of his or her clients half the attention, then the job will only be half as good.

When that happens, you get worse results. Clients won't be happy. The experience will be bad. They're not going to come back to that cleaning service, and they're going to tell other people not to use that cleaning service.

What happens with most traditional businesses or service businesses is they scale up to a particular point, and then they hit an invisible ceiling.

When they hit that, there is nothing they can do to go beyond. Every effort they make to try and go beyond it actually hurts them, because for every additional customer or client they're bringing on, they're crippling their chances of success.

Let's say for every twenty clients, the cleaning company makes one hundred grand. If you increase it to forty, you might make two hundred. Then you might make it eighty, and you only make a little bit more. This model of growth is linear. It doesn't matter what you try and do with linear growth. Eventually, you're going to hit a point where you just can't make any more money, even if you keep doing more and more work. It will reach a point where you actually start to go backward.

Creating a digital course is the opposite of this because the more customers you have, the more success stories you create, the more people you impact, the more your word of mouth grows, the more successful you will be. You can serve all of your customers in your private group at once, and for those who are hyper-successful, you can create an inner circle for $20k or $50k a year, or even more!

By creating a course from the start, with proper due diligence and testing, with your proof of concept, you are essentially skipping all of the steps it takes other people and other businesses years to figure out. You're going directly to the most profitable and most scalable method of business.

I have a plumber friend who used to do consultations for handyman businesses on how to find work fixing things inside of people's homes. When he was doing it, he was making $100k a year. He was stressed out though because he couldn't grow beyond that point; he was maxed out. He couldn't get on a plane more often. He couldn't do phone calls more often. He was at his limit. Then he moved to the online course model.

His first month after making his course, he started making ten grand a month while working fewer hours. Previously, he was working fifty hours a week for consultations and making $100,000 a year. With this model, he was working ten hours a week, but he started to make $120,000 a year with an infinite upside because he could now advertise his digital product (which never runs out of stock). The benefits go on and on. In a short amount of time, he took what he was making per year and started making it per month, doing the same amount of work. The only way that can happen is when you move to the knowledge economy.

People love self-service. How much easier is it for you to go on Amazon and buy something than it would be to actually call a business up and have a phone conversation with someone? Most people would prefer to go to a website and do it all self-service, never talk to anyone, and have the package just arrive. Same with your clients. Most people don't want to spend time talking and having meetings. They want a self-service solution where they can look at it and get the results quickly in their own time. That's what this new model allows you to do. Don't think, "Oh, I'm afraid of moving to this new model, because I think my clients' results will get worse." Truthfully, all I've seen is that they get better.

You know the reward you get from helping a client get the results they want one-on-one? Imagine seeing that same transformation happening without you doing anything. There is nothing quite like it.

Infinite Scale

Time is truly the one universal constant. Have you ever *actually thought* about why some people have more money than others, while we all have the exact same amount of time?

The answer is because some people work toward automation and infinite scale, while others cripple themselves by only making money by doing things that require them to physically be there or manually doing something.

The key to breaking the cycle is to create systems and automations that earn you money while you sleep. The inherent problem is that most people want immediate gratification, and this has been exponentiated by the widespread adoption of smartphones and social media.

When I created my first course, I created content, helped people one-on-one, made blog posts, Facebook posts, YouTube videos, and helped people in large Facebook groups. I started quietly collecting emails and building my Facebook group for three full months before I ever made a dollar. Then I made millions due to the compound interest I had been accumulating over those months!

It's critical to understand the concept of infinite scale and compound interest.

Infinite Scale: When you can sell something an infinite number of times and never run out of inventory, and something, with enough optimization, that you can put $1 of advertising into, and take $2 out!

Compound Interest: All of your incremental effort adds up and grows exponentially, slowly at first, but then explosively. Most people give up before they ever reach the explosive point where the culmination of all the compound interest is paid back in troves.

To further illustrate this, there's a guy from North Carolina whom I can almost guarantee you've never heard of named James Goodnight. He's worth 8.7 billion dollars. The average salary in America is $50,000.

Imagine making that. That is over $24 million per day. That means he makes $24 million on sick days and on Christmas. If he's hung over or takes a day off, he still makes $24,000,000 in a day.

James built up an invincible amount of incremental actions and did so focusing on the right things for years. Then the compound interest paid off beyond his wildest imagination!

Most people aren't willing to put in the upfront work developing systems and email automation, and building their tribe and passionate following, and adding a massive amount of value for free, before they ever even have anything to sell!

This is so critical to understand and cement the expectation in your head. Everyone who wants to create a massive course must put in the work to become known in the market and add value for free.

You become the iceberg. No one sees the work and value you add for 3-6 months; they just see the money you make when you release your course!

The Platinum Link

The most critical thing to understand about the universal constant, time, is something I call the Platinum Link in the value chain, and why ignoring everything else makes you rich.

Let me give an example to illustrate:

The airline industry is wildly profitable or unprofitable and a lot of work, depending on which link in the chain your business is in.

Online booking sites like Expedia.com take a larger portion of flight ticket cost than the airport (who does all of the work, employs all the staff, owns and pays for all the real estate and buildings, etc.).

There is a saying that the best way to become a millionaire is to be a billionaire and buy an airline because they're terrible money makers.

The Platinum Link in the value chain is not airports or airlines, it's the booking sites that sell the tickets on the internet.

You might be wondering how the booking sites make more than these massive airlines that own all these assets. The reason is that the world has changed. Like I mentioned previously, in the not too distant past, you built wealth by accumulating physical assets. The more you owned, the richer you were.

However, in today's day and age, reach and attention equates to wealth. The more people who are interested in what you have to say, the more wealthy you will become.

This is just the beginning of the knowledge economy. We have officially entered the information age. Now it is more important than ever to understand the value chain of your niche.

If your niche is travel, for example, spending your time focusing on creating an airline would not be the ideal section of the value chain; it would be focusing on creating the booking site because you would control the attention, reach, and distribution!

Taking the time to map out the Platinum Link, or the highest ROI section of the value chain, is always something you want to understand deeply.

I will give you another example to really hammer this home. When we were thinking about what type of Amazon software to create, we saw a million different offers. There was inventory forecasting software, split testing software, accounting software, the list goes on and on.

Instead of jumping in and creating a competitor to one of those, I broke down the Amazon niche into the things that are absolutely necessary for every new seller, because marketing towards beginners is always the most profitable with courses and software alike—because it represents the largest market.

There are profit drivers, and there is everything else. A profit driver is something that makes your customer more money.

Everything else would be something like accounting software that might be necessary for larger sellers but doesn't directly add value and is not applicable at all to beginners, since they're simply trying to start and have no need for accounting!

So, I broke down the three profit drivers that every beginner seller needs: Product Research, Keyword Research, and Launching your product to page one.

From there, I realized that creating product research software requires a huge amount of processing power, servers, infrastructure, and coding to analyze millions of Amazon products, but I found that it is actually relatively easy to build keyword and launch software that works.

So, I found the Platinum Link in my niche and built those two pieces of software with a lot of premeditated thought. They both were immediately successful!

Freeing Up Time

Whether you own an airline or work at the airport or own a travel booking site, time still passes, you still work 9-5. This is why you need to get a virtual assistant as soon as possible to free up your time to do more valuable things.

If you find yourself wasting time managing a Facebook group or generating leads for your business, or responding to emails, or finding graphic artists, or whatever—get a virtual assistant to help. It's the best use of money possible if you find the right one.

You may not feel like you need one now, but VA's can help immensely with building and moderating your Facebook group, editing videos, graphic design, etc. The person who tries to do everything themselves fails. The person who outsources intelligently wins. However, I always recommend learning things before you outsource them, so you know if they're being done correctly.

The Ultimate Time Saver—Digital Courses

You can either own a bakery and have staff and cost of ingredients for all the baked goods you sell, some of which go bad and have to be thrown away, OR you could teach thousands of people from around the world how to create a profitable bakery (which is entirely digital, requires no staff, has no spoilage, and has an infinitely scalable upside)!

That's how you want to think. When you're in business, you don't want to try and own all of the different links in the value chain. You want to own the platinum one and let everyone else handle the rest, because the rest is typically more headache than it is benefit and value.

Chapter 4
Sippin' on GIN and Juice: The Secret to Becoming a Millionaire

"Who controls the past controls the future;
who controls the present controls the past."
— George Orwell

Take Responsibility & Be Resilient

You have to realize where you are in life right now is because of nobody but you. The sooner you realize everything you think is someone else's fault is *yours*, the sooner your success will explode as an entrepreneur!

It goes against the grain to say things like "Everything is your fault" and "Wherever you are in life right now is because of nobody but you."

You might be thinking to yourself, "I thought this book was supposed to motivate me and make me feel good!"

This book only has one purpose: to give you a roadmap to earth-shattering improvements in your life and in your business.

While saying everything is perfect and dandy might make you feel better at a given moment, in the long run, it's only feeding the sympathy addiction our society has made mainstream. It's only going to make you suffer for longer because all that sympathy is doing is feeding your addiction, it's feeding the story that everything is going to be okay if you are the victim your whole life, and that where you are in life is someone else's fault. This is what people do when they blame other people for their own circumstances, and then they go out looking for sympathy, or they blame other things—they say it's the government's fault, or their boss, or their teachers, or their family or friends, or spouse. They want to believe their current situation is not their fault, and they want to be with people who believe that it's not their fault too because it feels better, and it's easier to blame someone or something else than to take ownership.

If you look around right now, what you have, what you own and the physical shape you're in, the mental state you're in, the cleanliness and tidiness of your home, your car, and how much money is in your bank account are all things you made happen.

It was all you. People's lives are exactly how they designed them to be. A lot of people often forget this. The person who you are now, you designed. If it's not something you're totally comfortable with, or if you were hoping to be in a better situation, then somewhere along the way, you must have been out of alignment. Your actions must have been out of alignment with what you really wanted to be.

When you take ownership of your life, nothing is unachievable; there is no failure, only feedback. If something doesn't work, it's simply feedback you'll apply to the next experiment. When your worldview and paradigm changes, you unlock your true potential.

Reverse Engineering

Part of taking ownership of your life is setting goals, but most people do it frontwards. The only way to set a goal meaningfully is by setting it backwards.

I like to plan month one from the end to the beginning, because you can think about your goals, but it won't happen until you reverse engineer it by working backward, turning it into daily tasks that will incrementally get you closer to achieving your goal.

What will the next thirty days look like for you? After seeing 10,000+ people pass through my programs, I can honestly say there is one thing the people who go on to have wild success have that no one else does.

They don't have one foot in eCom, one foot in their 9-5, and one foot in competitive poetry. They commit to creating the best digital course on the planet. They aren't frazzled and scattered. Their focus is pinpoint accurate, they set their mind to it, and they get to work. They don't just learn and watch videos, then drift back into Instagram and Netflix; they do the work.

30 Day Oath

The thing ALL my most successful students share is what I like to call the 30 Day Oath. What the 30 Day Oath means is that for the first 30 days of trying this stuff out, from choosing a niche to creating their Facebook group and posting content, reaching out to interested people in large Facebook groups, and making YouTube content, they gave it EVERYTHING THEY HAD.

They usually take about a week or two to get through all of the material, take notes, and think things through; they don't rush. Once they've learned the material, they take action and give it everything they've got!

While the average person dips their toes in, has a backup plan, and is planning on refunding if they don't see it work with one Facebook message or their first YouTube video, my millionaire students have burned their bridges and boats and are 150%

committed in every way, shape, and form.

What is interesting to see is that people who quit before 30 days NEVER end up achieving anything. Remember, your mindset creates your success. The same mindset which caused them to give up before 30 days bleeds into every area of their lives. People don't have business problems, they have personal problems that *manifest* in their business!

People who take consistent action for the first 30 days typically continue to take consistent action for the 30 days after that because they've started to shatter some of their lazy habits and have dramatically altered their worldview and definition of success. Whatever someone does for the first week typically is what they will do for the first 30 days, and whatever someone does for the first 30 days is typically what they will do for the 30 days after that, and the next year.

Habits

How you do things in the present is how you did them in the past and is how you will do things in the future.

Without changing your habits, you create more of the same in the present and more of the same in the future. It's not just linear, it's often exponential. The more you look toward the past and follow the patterns of the past, the more you dredge up those memories, and you have negative emotions and negative thoughts.

People who create real meaningful success in their lives take full responsibility for their results in life. They do not blame anyone else or play the victim. People who are victims get nothing in life. You don't want to be a victim saying it's the president's fault or your internet connection. Those people are saying that life is out of their control. They're in the pinball machine of life, bouncing around with no purpose or direction, and whatever happens to them, happens. You don't want to be a pinball.

Think about it like this…

You say, "I want to start my own course."

You call your friend and say, "Hey I'm thinking of starting my own course," and your friend says, "No, that's a stupid idea, you shouldn't do that."

Then you say, "Wow, you're right, I shouldn't do this."

That is facing resistance and choosing to quit.

Have you ever felt that everything just seems to go against you sometimes? What is that looming dark presence that just seems to make things not go your way? I used to always think like this. A car would run through a puddle, and I would get splashed just before work. I would get so upset and think "Why does this stuff always happen to me, why do I deserve this?"

It became a mindset where I was always the victim, the world was against me, and no matter what I did, it seemed to be against me. My boss didn't like me as much as my co-workers; girls didn't want me as much as they wanted my friends. I was always the victim.

One of the biggest reasons my life changed, a complete 180° for the better, was because I flipped my mentality on this exact idea. I realized it wasn't the world that was against me.

It was me.

Blaming other people or scenarios or external influences was the fastest way to ensure I never got what I wanted because it *relieved* me of the responsibility of improving. When I realized and accepted that what was happening in my life was my fault, and the only way to change it was one day at a time, with intentional, focused movement towards my goal, everything changed.

All of a sudden when something didn't go my way, instead of feeling sorry for myself, I analyzed WHY it didn't go my way and made adjustments and self-reflected.

The best indicator of this sense of ownership is the market. The market is very accurate at rewarding the participants who hustle, are consistently taking action, and who deserve things and the market is very accurate at NOT rewarding anyone who doesn't. Think about it: if people go to college and get a degree and they CAN'T get a job or make any money, it's a sign that something is off and something's gotta give.

It's Impossible to Grow without Facing Resistance

The great masters of all time learned to observe their lives as a series of never-ending experiments. With each experiment, they reflected on the outcome and learned from it. If they started a business and failed, they analyzed it with scrutinizing detail and grew stronger, instead of the majority of people who fail and then implode, get down on themselves and feel like they will never make it.

Don't Be Afraid to Make Mistakes

As we progress, we make mistakes. We burn our hands on the stove, and we get feedback that says "Okay, don't touch the stove again." It's feedback, not failure. We don't stop cooking; we don't give up, even if it's painful. We learn, and think to ourselves, "Next time, I'll know the stove is hot, so I won't touch it."

A person who continually reflects on things and searches for what "truth" is lives a seriously next-level life. The problem is that when most people in the world experience misfortune, instead of taking responsibility for it and learning from it, they blame something or someone else.

Once you do enough of that, your own life is no longer in your control. Now you're looking to someone else as the only means to create the life you want. It's the government's fault, your family's fault, your boss's fault. Whenever you put the blame on someone or something else, you become a victim.

Don't Make Excuses

Have you ever heard your friends or family say they want to start their own business or become an entrepreneur, but they just don't have enough time? In saying this, they are the victim of their schedule, not the master of it.

Have you ever caught yourself saying you don't have enough time to build a business? Let me break down exactly how illogical that is. If you create a business the right way, an automated, scalable business (like a digital course), then starting a business does not take time, it makes time.

If you think you don't have enough time, then I want you to track, down to the minute, what you do in an average day, and I bet you'll be surprised by what makes up that time.

When you learn to obliterate the victim mentality, the direct causality between your actions and the effects of your actions becomes clear. When you work smarter consistently, you get the outcome you want faster. When you blame others for your problems and situations, you get nothing but excuses.

Successful entrepreneurs face their fears, own their problems, and take accountability for their results, whether bad or good.

Facing the music is when you stop running away from the pain and problems in your life by avoiding them and distracting or sedating yourself. A lot of people ignore things. They won't answer calls or emails from a particular person. They've got a problem with a relationship, and they won't fix it. They just sweep it under the rug.

At the beginning of my entrepreneurial journey, when things got bad for me, I would just stay in bed and hide. When I woke up, I knew I had to go out and face the day, make calls, and get out of my comfort zone. A way of escaping that was just to stay asleep. Another avoidance tactic was going out with friends and drinking alcohol. After I had a few drinks, I forgot about the things that were worrying me. These were ways of escaping.

If someone is too afraid to step outside of their comfort zone, it means they're judging people who are stepping outside of their comfort zone. The only way to be free of the fear, so you can step outside your comfort zone, is to stop judging other people who do it.

It's really as simple as that. It will change everything for you. From this point on, you do not want to judge anyone. You want to let go of all of those feelings and labels you've given to people. Then you will be totally invincible and able to do anything you want to without fear.

The GIN Mentality

There two types of people in the world. The type of person you are dictates your success.

Person A: I don't know how to make a course…

Person B: I don't know how to make a course…YET!

GIN is an acronym for GOOGLE IT NOW!

One of the most profound, startling revelations I've made going from nothing to eight figures in eighteen months is that the difference between millionaires and everyone else is a slightly greater willingness to GIN (Google It Now).

I know that sounds simple—but if you get NOTHING else from this entire book and truly buy into this one idea, you will become a millionaire with enough consistency and smart work, I guarantee you that.

YouTube and Google have tutorials on <u>**EVERYTHING.**</u>

If you happen to get stuck building a membership site, or creating your first email campaign, or any number of countless things, remember the GIN mentality. You MUST catch yourself when you think, "I don't know how to _____."

Simply Google it. You are in the top 1% now; you can learn and do anything. You are not a victim, and even if you don't yet have the resources, you have the resourcefulness!

Think about it this way, just a few short years ago, if you didn't know something, you needed to go to school, read an encyclopedia, or just guess until you figured it out.

Now all the information from history is quite **LITERALLY** at your fingertips, yet people still find excuses not to figure out how to do things. But not you, not anymore!

Chapter 5

Uncovering Your Perfect Niche

How to Find the Perfect Name for Your Course

The best way to name your course is to look at examples of proven course titles and reverse engineer your own course name from that. You want to use something that is three words or less, describes what your course is about, and generates interest. Think about your customers. Maybe they want a profit engine, to know the secrets behind making a digital course, or the underground info on getting six-pack abs!

- Digital Course Secrets
- Lean Belly Breakthrough
- Profit Engine
- Writing to Wealth
- Fat Decimator Blueprint
- Underground 6-Pack Blueprint
- Zero to Launch
- Idea to Exit
- Scrawny to Brawny
- Product Launch Formula
- Yes Engine

- Spirit Junkie Masterclass
- Trust Machine
- Advanced Marketing Masterclass
- How to Ditch Sugar
- Body Language Sells

It is an added bonus if your course forms an easy to remember acronym like DCS, which stands for Digital Course Secrets. People will start to refer to your course by that acronym. When you are creating a movement, this makes a difference!

You also want to have a specific outcome:

- Lose 10 pounds
- Get your first 10,000 followers
- Start earning profit selling on Amazon

You don't want to make specific claims about money (because of paid traffic requirements and liability), so don't say "Make $100,000 in a month guaranteed!" Be general enough and allow people to infer their desired results to protect yourself from liability, and to comply with Facebook and Google landing page requirements and the FTC.

The Basic Formula that always works is "**Desired Result**, Even if (**Objection 1, Objection 2, Objection 3**)"

For example, "How to Sell on Amazon and Earn a Full-Time Income, Even if You Have No Experience Selling Online, No Technical Skills, and Barely Any Money to Start!"

Your Course Name Checklist for Success:

- Is it easy to remember?
- Are there any keywords that your audience will immediately recognize?
- Is the URL available?
- Is it easy to say out loud?
- Is it generally clear what it is you do?

Taming the Niche

Sometimes the best way to get things done is with some old-fashioned numbered lists. There have been countless studies and science backing the simple truth that numerical organization calms and focuses the mind. Below is an excellent way to get the ball rolling. Don't overthink these, literally just starting writing or typing—GO!

1. List 3 niches you know, have experience with, or are passionate about.
2. List 3 skill sets you currently have.
3. List the fears of the niches you selected (What keeps them up at night?)
4. List the desires of the niches you selected (What are their secret desires they want more than anything?)
5. Select the most powerful fear and desire and use that to take them from their current situation to their desired situation.

If you don't feel you have enough expertise yet to be able to help others, don't worry, you now have the **GIN** mentality, which means you can learn anything you set your mind to. When you focus all your attention on becoming really good at one thing, you'll be surprised at how fast you become an expert at that one thing!

People are getting pulled in 100 different directions every day all day long, and if you have the willpower to focus all your attention on mastering one skill, and specializing in that skill (which falls within Health, Wealth, or Relationships), you can become an expert faster than you think!

At the end of the day, all you really need to have is the moral obligation to commit to becoming an expert at whatever you choose to create your course about!

Know Your Audience

The more you know and understand your audience, the better! Past success can be a predictor of future success. If your customers are engineers, then you'd want to make sure the way you present your course is very analytical and logical.

How one person says something does not always equate to all the ways to say something. When you go to create YouTube videos and content, remember that if you can get someone interested in related subjects, you can get them interested in your course! Always think outside the box!

For example, let's say I want to make an Amazon course. I can attract attention in 1,000 other ways on YouTube with complementary content.

How to make money online; how to make $100 a day; how to be motivated; how to manage your time better; what is passive income? The opportunities are endless.

Have you ever achieved anything in life that other people may want help achieving too? Maybe you lost weight. Maybe you decluttered your life. Maybe you figured out the best way to store spices in a cabinet. It could be anything.

What type of success have you already had?

It can be a big success or a small success. As an example, maybe you helped your kid study for a math test, and they got an A. What did you do to help them?

Believe it or not, that could be a course, too. You can teach parents how to teach their kids how to study.

I want you to think through some of the successes you've had in your life thus far. Go year by year. Remember: it doesn't have to be a huge success. It can be any success. Ideally, something you think someone else would be interested in as well.

What do people ask you for advice or help about?

Do you see someone else selling an online course and think to yourself: "I can do that, too!" or "I can do that better!"?

The biggest reason startups and businesses fail is NOT because of their products, customer service, or cash flow. It is because they create something people don't want or need.

Have courses been created on your specific topic? This doesn't have to be a "yes" if you can answer "yes" to a few other questions I'm going to ask you. However, it is a big red flag if nobody is teaching on the topic you want to teach. It's not a make or break type of thing because you might be the first to move forward with it, and you might just crush it.

Have books been written on your specific topic?

Maybe there are no courses out about your topic yet, but perhaps there are some books. It is ideal to make sure there is some material out there already. Of course, there's not going to be material out there exactly the way you want to teach it. We're just talking about the general topic.

If **Yes**—look for 3 or 4-star reviews on Amazon and look for commonalities. Remember 5 stars are usually fantastic things, and 1 star means the book spontaneously combusted in the person's hand, so focus on the articulate, meaningful feedback!

Have blog posts been written on your specific topic?

If you have a viable topic that people really want and need, you will usually find a handful of blog posts have already been written about the topic. That is a good thing. You definitely need some blog posts, books, and ideally, a few courses. That would be the perfect situation to know that if you move forward, there will be an audience that wants and needs what you are creating.

The most important thing is <u>YOU MUST</u> make a decision.

You're never going to have all the information to make the perfect decision. It is literally impossible to make a perfect decision. The human mind simply cannot compute all the data in the world to be able to make a perfect decision.

Don't fool yourself. Just pick a niche. You don't need to put that much thought into it because this is an iterative process where we test things and sometimes we have to change things around. There's no such thing as a wrong decision when you pick your course niche.

My first course started so rough. I was super anxious and doubtful when I launched it. This is what most people have to understand. No one starts out with an excellent offer and total confidence in their niche. Everything is going to feel imperfect. You're going to doubt your niche. You're going to doubt your offer. It's totally normal. It's healthy. It's how everyone has felt, including me.

Look at the information, give yourself a reasonable amount of time, make a decision, and then stick to it. Eventually, you're going to get enough feedback from your proof of concept and minimum viability exercises (I'll teach these later on) to figure out whether you should change it up or stick to it. Do not allow yourself to overcomplicate things. You just need to trust the process, trust yourself, and do the work. If you do all of that, then everything will happen for you.

Chapter 6

One Question to Rule Them All

One Question to Bind Them

Whatever your main idea for a course, say to yourself, "Will my course about 'BLANK' give my customers their desired results (make more money, lose weight, find the woman of my dreams) from A-Z even if they're a complete beginner with no experience?"

If the answer is yes, and your course falls under the **3 pillars: Health, Wealth, and Relationships**, you might have found your idea!

Remember, even if there are courses currently in your niche, you can win by caring more, designing a better course, and being more active helping your students one-on-one (something your students value more than anything). Also, the current people in your space may start doing other things, stop updating their course, etc. There is always more room in evergreen niches for the right person, ALWAYS!

Remember you can make a course on anything. Here are a few awesome examples…

I.   Jacob Hiller made a course on how to JUMP HIGHER and transitioned that business into a multimillion-dollar empire!

II. Jermaine Griggs made a course on how to play piano by ear; he monetized his love for piano by teaching and inspiring others to do the same!

III. Robert Allen made a course on how to buy real estate with little or no money down and has often stated that he made millions in real estate and hundreds of millions teaching it!

Once you have clients, the best way to determine your point of difference is to private message them on Facebook or send them an email and ask them why they purchased from you instead of somebody else. You can also ask them on the phone. If you have clients, you must do this, as the feedback you get from this will be worth millions to you in the long run.

What do you think Jacob Hiller's friends told him when he decided to quit his job to focus on a core product teaching people how to jump higher? They probably said he was crazy, and told him to do the smart thing, have a backup plan, and keep his 9-5 job.

To Succeed, You Must First Begin

One of the best lessons I've learned as an entrepreneur is that it doesn't matter what is "true," what matters is what you believe to be true because with enough consistent, focused actions, it will become true.

That sentence is one of the most important things I could possibly teach you, so I'm going to write it again. Print it out, get a tattoo on your forehead, write it in permanent marker on your laptop screen, whatever you need to do...

"It doesn't matter what is true, what matters is what you believe to be true because with enough consistent, focused actions, it will become true."

We have our beliefs and our reality, and with enough consistent smart work, our beliefs become our reality. If our current reality isn't what we want, then we are doomed UNLESS we change our belief about it.

We have to take action. Thoughts, on their own, won't do anything. We need to have a thought, and then we need to take action.

You need to have belief. You need to take action. Then you need to make it come into existence. Finally, you need to listen to the feedback and adjust the beliefs and actions.

Your belief is just as important as your actions. As my beliefs are growing, my actions are growing, and as my actions are growing, my confirmed reality is growing. As my confirmed reality is growing, my beliefs are growing. Everything is feeding off each other in an invincible upward feedback cycle of unstoppable confidence and power.

Once you believe you can do something, you start taking massive actions because you believe it. Then you start experiencing reality.

The Fab 5 of Financial Freedom

To summarize and evaluate your course idea in the most succinct way, I created the Fab 5 of Financial Freedom. Talk about alliteration!

The Fab 5 is meant to evaluate your idea with real-world data and resources. If these resources ever disappear in the chaos of life, there will be other similar resources you can use in their place.

1. Does it fall into one of the Evergreen 3 pillars (**Health, Wealth, Relationships**)?

2. Can you show **proof** of a similar course that has been successful?

3. Can you show **proof** of YouTube videos with at least 25,000 views or more on the subject? On multiple related topics? For example, if you're creating a course on Amazon, are there videos on product research, how to make a listing, seller central tutorials, or how to do PPC? You want multiple proven topics you can make videos about! Also, it's great to see books, ebooks, or blog posts on your course niche as well to prove that people are interested.

4. Can you show **proof** of Facebook groups, or Instagram accounts, or social media forums/communities about your course niche? The purpose here being to prove there are places where people interested in your niche congregate and can be reached!

5. Can you show the **top person** in your niche and their main social media or communication medium? Do they mainly communicate via a YouTube channel, Instagram page, blog, their sales page, or a webinar?

Take the top five courses that are most similar to what you want to create and look at what they charge to find an average of what you could potentially charge for your course starting out.

And if you want feedback on your course idea and to be around other successful entrepreneurs building digital courses—I suggest you join our Facebook community…

I suggest doing it right now, before you forget. It only takes thirty seconds. Go to Facebook on your phone or computer, type "**Digital Course Secrets**" into the search bar, and join our public group!

Remember:

DO NOT try to force your course idea if it doesn't fit

DO NOT fall in love with your passion project

DO NOT be blinded by your own personal opinions

<u>DO</u> interpret and use the data you collect from this book to select a course that will add value to people, and in doing so, make you money!

Being emotionally attached to a course idea that doesn't fit the data is the surest way to waste a ton of your time and fail miserably.

Continuous Improvement

I want you to make a commitment to me and, most importantly, to yourself!

You can have financial freedom, or you can have excuses, but you can't have both. This book is not only about making a course, becoming financially free, and impacting and helping others, it's also about growing as a person.

A vital part of that is what I like to call "continuous improvement." There WILL be times when you feel overwhelmed, in over your head, or technologically challenged, but if it were easy, then everyone would do it.

What continuous improvement means is each day you get a little better. Doing ten minutes of niche research one day and fifteen the next, or researching one YouTube video one day and two the next. The point is never let yourself have *ZERO DAYS*. You always have to do something, and the incremental gains of doing things, learning, and getting better every single day will completely change your life. It might not happen overnight, but it <u>WILL</u> happen!

If you're stuck at any stage or you're doubting yourself, it's natural, but learn to be reflective, stop and say to yourself, what is the question that I need answered? How can I ask a question to get over my doubt or fear?

Look beyond the information you're being taught. Look at what your teachers are DOING. I want you to start *noticing* what I'm doing, because it's important to not only learn from the book material but also to learn from the book itself as an example.

Micro Commitments

When you create your course, it's essential for people to feel involved, part of your team and family, and that they belong. It is human nature to stay quiet in groups until you believe you have been given a chance to speak. It is your responsibility as a course creator to make everyone feel welcome.

Start with simple worksheets and checklists. Make summaries for your students to make things as easy as possible. I get people to start with some simple worksheets to get some micro commitments.

Always keep momentum in mind. Momentum is a very real thing. The example I like to use to illustrate this is a merry-go-round. You push and push, and it's tough to get started and takes all your effort, but once the wheel gets going, it spins effortlessly!

The same is true with your students in your course!

Once someone has done one small thing, they're more likely to do a larger thing. Don't burden them immediately. Reel them in with more and more commitment. Get people a win ASAP. Get people a client as quickly as possible, if that's what you're trying to do. If you're trying to help people lose weight, get them to follow a routine as quickly as possible. Get them some form of feedback ASAP such as a paying client, feeling healthier, or a date. Once they see that, they're hooked.

When you fill out checklists, get your first client through FB messages, LinkedIn, or from a FB group, those are quick wins. As soon as your customers see the power of your system and your teachings, they will be 100x more likely to succeed!

Chapter 7
Remastered Worldview: How Your Paradigms Shape Your Life

There is a parable from ancient India about blind men and an elephant. It is a story about a group of blind men who had never come across an elephant before, and who learn about and conceptualize what the elephant is like by touching it. Each blind man feels a different part of the elephant's body, but only one part, such as the side or the tusk. They describe the elephant based on their limited experience, and their descriptions of the elephant are wildly different from each other.

The parable implies that one's subjective experience can be true, but that experience is inherently limited by its failure to account for other truths or the totality of truth.

So why is this important? Because it illustrates your beliefs are subjective. There is no absolute truth; it's only your perception of reality. We tend to believe that everybody thinks the same way we do. We think if we think something, then everyone thinks the same, or if we believe in something, then everyone believes in it.

Successful people see, think, and believe totally different things than people who fail do.

I want to share with you a personal story to illustrate this.

When I was at PricewaterhouseCoopers, I was seen as a massive success in my family; five hundred people applied for one prestigious space at PwC.

I grew up in a working-class family, with hard-working parents who loved and supported me but thought the only "right path" was to get a 9-5 job, fit in, and save for retirement. My view of success was to go to college, get a stable job, and max out my 401k contributions.

I met someone I will call "Lady Luck" because thousands of people have read this book, and I want to keep her privacy intact. Her dad was ridiculously wealthy, like tennis-court-basketball-court-bowling alley-in-the home wealthy. The first time I saw her parents' house, it completely changed my worldview, my paradigm, how I perceived the world, and what I considered to be success. Previously, I thought $55,000 a year for a 23-year-old was terrific. If you make $100k, you're wealthy. That is what I thought success was.

I thought to be wealthy you had to get a job. Those beliefs, that paradigm and worldview, were embedded in my brain from my childhood growing up in a traditional home. Don't get me wrong, I love my parents with all my heart, but they were conventional. They believed in responsibility and were risk averse because they had to take care of my sister and me.

I arrived at this massive palace with "Lady Luck," and my idea of success was totally shattered. My entire worldview I had accumulated over years evaporated instantly.

My entire life growing up, my dad would follow me around and turn off the TV, lights, and the heater or air conditioner when I left rooms because he wanted to conserve energy when we weren't using it. He was obsessed with it, and I don't necessarily blame him. Why waste energy?

Logically, it makes sense not to waste energy, but this family had massive light structures and fountains, things that used vast amounts of energy that were always on. They did that because they wanted to enjoy it, and I remember saying, "You're not supposed to do that, you're wasting energy." Her dad, who owned the house, said he wasn't wasting energy, he was enjoying it.

I knew then that he was not an average person. I'd never really met someone this different before. Since meeting him, something about me had changed too. I began questioning things. I began to think, "What else have I got wrong here? I mean, what else does this guy know that I don't know?"

I started to think about this. It was the first time I really questioned what I was doing in my existence and everything. When I got back to my cubicle at PwC where I used to be happy, now I was questioning if this was what I was meant for. This couldn't be my destiny. I had been led to believe this was the definition of success, and that is what I had believed.

But coming back from this palace and witnessing true abundance for the first time, I started to panic, and I texted "Lady Luck" immediately and asked what her dad did. She told me he started his own business and was an entrepreneur.

At that moment in my life, I knew what I wanted; the light bulb was officially on and shining brightly. I knew I needed to make a change and find my destiny. Similar to how that was the moment for me, where I knew what I needed to do, let this moment, and *Unfair Advantage* be the moment for you. You can change your worldview and begin the next chapter of your life.

📖 Part 1 Summary

- You learned how to choose an always profitable evergreen course topic (health, wealth, relationships).
- You learned how to choose a simple, memorable name for your course with an acronym.
- You learned how to choose a catchphrase indicating how your customers can get their desire without their common objections.
- You learned how to choose your personal brand name, and I suggested a personal brand as it has more longevity, and if you have a difficult to pronounce name choosing a pseudonym such as Kevin David.

✓ Part 1 Checklist

- What are your evergreen course niche topic and sub-niche? (Health, Wealth, Relationships)
- What is your course name?
- What is your catchphrase?
- What is your brand name or personal brand?
- Have you answered the Fab 5 questions?

The rest of *Unfair Advantage* is jam-packed with the information you need to start creating your course, but if you're ready to skip straight to the end of the line and start your Digital Course movement today, I suggest taking a look at our free training available for a limited time at www.digitalcoursesecrets.com/go

Part 2
Building Your Tribe

Chapter 8

The Lone Wolf:
Stop Following the Crowd

"We find comfort among those who agree with us -
growth among those who don't."
— Frank A. Clark

False Universal Truths

A lot of people have already formed false universal truths. They think because they tried Facebook ads and it didn't work, Facebook ads never work. Or they heard from a friend of a friend once that it is too late to start YouTube, so YouTube must be too saturated.

I want you to understand how unbelievably crazy those assumptions are.

Someone who's just getting started and doesn't know what they are doing is telling themselves universally and unequivocally that since Facebook ads didn't work once for them, they must not work under any circumstances for anyone. Then how do other people make so much money with Facebook ads? How do people create business empires and form massive followings with YouTube?

Trust the process, do the work, and you will get results. Let yourself be affected by the hivemind and influenced by the crowd, and you'll always be silent and obedient. Listen to what the majority of people say, and you'll get the same results as the majority of people.

Have you ever worked at a corporate job and thought to yourself that the way reports were processed was wildly inefficient?

People are often mentally trapped doing things the way they've always been done, rather than making obvious and basic improvements.

When you ask a lot of businesses, "Why are you still doing that?" they respond, "Well, that's the way it's always been done." I remember when I was an accountant, one of my clients was still using paper books to keep their accounts rather than accounting software. They had lost certain sheets and expenses; it was a mess. I asked why on earth they were doing things this way, and they responded that was just the way things had always been done.

People believe that if *everybody* believes something, or if everybody is doing something a certain way, then it must be right. When I was growing up, everyone went to high school, then college, and then got a job. So, I thought that is what I should do. I spent tens of thousands of dollars to learn antiquated information, most of which was wildly irrelevant to the real world, only to come out when I graduated offensively underprepared for what the world was really like. Damn, why did I listen to everyone?

When I quit my job, everyone told me I needed to save for retirement, have a backup plan and a degree. It was hard to believe I was right when everyone else in my life: my parents, my family, my friends, my girlfriend, my coworkers said I was wrong. However, I believed in myself, and I went against the grain and forged my own path.

I ended up making a fortune having the best time of my life and creating fortunes for thousands of my students. The problem is people want to fit in with social circles and adjust their behavior accordingly. People don't want to stir the pot and cause conflict or be disowned, so they never question anything. Without realizing it, they join the pack and attack anyone who questions the collective beliefs of the group.

When I said I was quitting my job to become an entrepreneur, everyone said, "Oh gosh Kevin, are you sure? I don't want you to get your hopes up, don't you know that 87% of business fail? Are you sure? I just don't want to see you get hurt. Do you have a backup plan?"

Then all of a sudden...

BOOM! your business explodes, and all your friends and family say, "I knew you'd be successful!"

It would be easy to be resentful, but I don't blame anyone for any of it. I still love them all. The point is that you will always have people in the hivemind who question things you do. It's critical to BE READY FOR THAT, and be ready for the fact that they're going to push against you and your progress as an entrepreneur. It is essential that you form your own viewpoints, question everything, and become an independent thinker.

Question Everything

Think for yourself and avoid the biased, delusional hivemind influencing most of society and maintaining the status quo. If you want to be successful, make a ton of money, and live a beautiful life where you hold the steering wheel, you must become a reflective, experimental researcher of your own life.

Participants just get stepped on. Participants get nothing. You have to learn to become an experimenter, a researcher, a reflector, and most importantly, an intelligent, consistent implementer.

When I started with my course, all internet marketers said you need to have one flagship course; everyone does, that's how it's done.

You need to do big joint ventures and affiliates. That's the only way you make money. You need to have an office with a bunch of employees, and you need to do things the right way.

I figured out a lot of people were just flat out wrong, and the people who taught Facebook, YouTube, and Google ads were flat out wrong. When I started questioning things, I could not believe it. That's how I started to get really good at things, because I no longer just followed what the crowd said and thought for myself. I figured things out properly and formed my own views.

You can be a wolf, or you can be a sheep, but you can't be both.

Chapter 9

Creating Your Movement: The Three Requirements

If you want to to "personally" consult people one-on-one without it taking up all of your time, this is best done with video. No matter how many times a video plays, it can keep playing a billion more times with no additional manual effort, and this is the truest form of efficiency!

To do this, you must connect with people on a personal level. Logic does not sell. Emotion sells, and logic justifies those purchase decisions.

To connect with people, you must become an attractive character—someone people look up to, respect, and want to become!

I first learned about the concept of the attractive character from an entrepreneur named Russell Brunson, and it completely changed my life. This idea has been around for years in one form or another, but it's a point worth noting that I first heard about it from Russell Brunson. I'm sure at one point he first heard about it in another form from someone else. That is the beauty of the knowledge economy, what matters is YOU teaching your audience important concepts with your own experiences and giving them "Aha!" moments that prompt them to change their life!

All marketing is just the recirculation and evolution of the same base principles. Similarly, you need to harness the power of the attractive character. Before you assume you're not an attractive character, read on, and remember, what you believe becomes real with enough consistent action.

1. ATTRACTIVE CHARACTER (YOU)

To properly market yourself from the beginning, you need to become the Attractive Character. The Attractive Character (YOU) has already gone from your customer's current situation to your customer's desired situation.

Maybe you went from someone who was trapped in their 9-5 job, depressed in your cubicle to traveling South East Asia, working from your laptop on the beach in Thailand living the life of your dreams.

Look back at your life and childhood and the negative things you experienced. Identify how you can turn those around to be lessons you're thankful for because they made you who you are today.

I wasn't born with a silver spoon in my mouth. I had to put in the work to be where I am today. I lacked experience or any entrepreneurial friends or family, and was told I was dumb at math in school and wouldn't achieve anything in my life. I was working eighty hours a week as a corporate drone. I was anxious and depressed. However, I'm thankful for all of this because it made me hungry to prove myself and make a stand towards reforming education and employment.

What events or milestones can you build into your story right now?

If you have a 9-5 job, take a photo of your cubicle, your desk, and your dress clothes. Make it as meaningful as possible because you'll be repeating it a lot as you grow, and your story is the most important thing! The closer people can compare their current situation to what yours once was, the better!

People relate to your story, and that is why they buy. You were in their shoes, and now you have the life they want.

I decided to start my own Amazon business and grew it up to $1,000/day within the first three months, and then quit my 9-5 job to go all in. For this, I could include a picture of me traveling through Asia.

I grew my eCommerce businesses to $50,000/month in the first year, moved out of my apartment, and into my dream home. I could include a picture of me buying a new car or showing a sales screenshot milestone.

Every good story has more or less the exact same underlying conflict: an interesting person who is pursuing a desire, who faced adversity and seemingly insurmountable obstacles but made it work.

The attractive character is confident, knowledgeable, and helpful; the attractive character is the person with the answers. Remember, you need to have the answers. If you don't know them now, use the GIN method—a basic willingness to Google is what makes millionaires.

2. FUTURE-BASED

Your movement and course topic need to be future-based. If you look at the campaign slogans of most successful presidential runs, you'll see they are future-based. Presidents win based on future hope. Losers lose because they try to improve.

For example, Obama's slogan was "The Change We Need," and Trump is well-known for his "Make America Great Again" campaign. Regardless of how you feel about politics, you can learn a lot from their messaging. Their marketing messages are brilliantly simple. There is a great deal to learn from the nuances of how they communicate their messages.

People need to BELIEVE the future can be different from their current situation. To get people to believe in something, and in you and your movement, it needs to be centered around the future. The idea of a new beginning in the future is much easier to stomach than the thought of the hard work and effort it takes to improve yourself now, especially in ways you've already tried and failed in the past.

3. NEW OPPORTUNITY

Your movement needs to not only be future-based but also branded as a new opportunity. People who are trying to lose weight have probably tried diets before and failed. They associate that failure with what they've already tried.

Creating a new opportunity generates EXCITEMENT instead of DREAD, which is vitally important to creating a successful movement. You need to have momentum and excitement on your side!

For your course, you want to find a sub-niche within an overarching niche, then present it as a new opportunity, not an improvement.

Improvement is 100x harder. It requires people to admit failure and realize the hardship to improve, which they've already tried and failed. A new opportunity allows them to see the end result and not the work!

This is important *psychologically* to your customers. The thought of improving something carries a burden of difficulty. They associate improvement of something they already understand (like their diet) as difficult and, therefore, naturally dread it.

Alternatively, if you present something as a brand new

opportunity (e.g., eat what you love and still lose weight using the brand new XYZ system), they associate this idea with excitement.

Starbucks came in and revolutionized America with fancy coffee. Now every American is queued up out the door to spend five bucks on a coffee. However, if you'd asked them this twenty years ago, no one would have imagined spending that much money on a coffee.

Starbucks was not just coffee, it was a brand new experience. It wasn't cheap coffee at a donut shop; it was bolder, richer, European coffee sold in a modern, inviting environment. They completely changed the baseline price and mentality about coffee.

This is the difference in thinking. You're not looking at something as it is. You're looking at what it is becoming.

Your New Opportunity

Who I am today is not who I was back when I was a 9-5 drone.

If you met me then and meet me now, we are totally different. One person was very judgmental; one person blamed everything other than himself. One person was immature and thought he could do nothing, make no effort at all, and expected the world in return.

The people who refuse to change anything about themselves and just want to make more money never make any money. The people who are open to change and improvement are making the most money.

Being outside of my comfort zone is my new comfort zone. For most people, they never want to go there; they resist leaving their comfort zone at all costs. What you believe becomes your reality. You are not just someone. You are always *becoming* someone. Your identity forms your reality. Because life is always moving, we can't live the life we desire without intent.

Chapter 10
Becoming the Creator

"They don't care how much you know until they
know how much you care."
— Anonymous

Asking the Right Questions

If you're not intentional about who you become and what your life becomes, you are just a pinball in the machine of life, bouncing around endlessly outside of your own control, and that is not where you want to be!

If you ask the question, "Who am I?", look at your current situation now, and it's not very good, then that belief confirms your reality. You need to change your beliefs, and instead of saying, "Who am I?", you need to ask the question, "Who am I becoming?"

Taking Action

You have to take action. Thoughts, on their own, won't do anything. Taking action requires being decisive. You can't worry and procrastinate forever about making decisions. One thing every successful person has in common is the ability to make large decisions quickly and accurately. I don't mean being irrational, I mean taking the information presented, evaluating it thoroughly, then making a decision. You have to make decisions; otherwise, you'll drown in mediocrity.

When I was looking for a house in San Diego, I looked at probably ten houses the first day. I knew none of them were MY house and never gave any of them a second thought. On the second day, I looked at one house, and I knew it was the one.

My real estate agent asked, "Are you sure; don't you want to see the rest of the houses I've lined up?" She was shocked because she had never seen someone make decisions like that, especially on a multimillion-dollar purchase. We looked at comps and made a fair offer an hour later.

The Three Types of Course Creators

As an expert/teacher/course creator you can fit into one of three categorizations, but what is CRITICAL for all three is that you are genuine. People can sense when someone is being genuine. More than any other reason, thousands of students who've bought my programs have done so because they said I seemed genuine and they could relate to me. This is incredibly important to understand.

It is also incredibly important to understand you do NOT need to be some world-class expert before you can begin helping others with your course. There are many shapes and sizes of course creators but generally, all course creators fall into one of three categories.

Course Creator #1—The Relatable Beginner

No credentials or experience, but teaches what he learns and what he knows, doesn't make any claims of success himself and doesn't make claims about his students, simply teaches what he knows and what he has learned himself.

This is a great way to start building your audience until you transition into one of the following two categories. People say to me all the time, "Kevin, I'd love to make a course, but I'm not an expert at anything." The truth is ALL experts started out as non-experts. You just have to make the decision to start.

Remember, you don't need to be an expert to be a good course creator. You have to know just enough *more* than your students for your course to be worth the money. You also have to care more and help them more than anyone else to be successful!

Course Creator #2—The Seasoned Pro

Has credentials, including advanced degrees, traditional job experience, and knows what he's talking about.

Of course, don't rub being an "expert" in people's faces, but share how you learned what you know in a likable way!

You can emphasize these credentials in the content you create to establish yourself as someone who knows what they're talking about. That credibility will help you maintain and attract attention!

Course Creator #3—The Results Getter

No traditional credentials or traditional experience, but has either helped themselves or others with their course topic. In reality, this can be the best positioning to be in.

No matter what you do—whether you're just getting started or you've been at it for a while—if you can position yourself as the person who gets results for other people, it doesn't matter if you're new and likable or if you have all the credentials in the world.

When your messages cause polarity, it attracts attention and people will pay for it.

Neutrality is boring. You have to have an opinion. Rarely is money made or change created when you stay neutral. Being polar is what attracts raving fans and people who follow you and pay for your advice.

If your audience thinks you are just in this to make money, your vehicle for change will not last long. If you genuinely believe in your message and it is useful and valuable to your clients, then you have a moral obligation to try to serve them in every way possible.

That is why I am so aggressive in my marketing, because I know if I can get people's attention, I really can change their lives. If you haven't offended someone by noon, then you're not marketing hard enough. You need to learn to have thick skin because when you start to get haters, it generally means you're doing something right!

Chapter 11

The "Just Do It" Mentality: Break Things Quickly

The Pareto Principle

With a finite number of hours in the day, and constant and continuous distractions in our lives, how do we decide what to spend our time on to produce the results we desire fastest?

The Pareto principle, also known as the 80/20 rule, is a theory maintaining that 80% of the output from a given situation or system is determined by 20% of the input. It's a law of nature that shows up in the world over and over again in all areas of life.

Why does 80/20 happen?

That's probably one of the most important questions in the world. It doesn't matter where you look. 80/20 presents itself everywhere because of the avalanche effect.

If you've ever been to a party, and one person leaves, all of a sudden everyone starts to leave. So, if a lot of people are joining the party, then it's going to start spiraling up, more people are joining, but as soon as people start leaving, it's going to start spiraling down. These things can spiral up or spiral down, depending on whether the feedback is positive or negative.

It's important to control this upward or downward trend in your life. Once you start building up a whole bunch of money, you begin to earn a lot of interest on that money. That affects more money in your bank account and feeds back on to the interest on all that money. It keeps spiraling up and up.

We see the same on the internet, like with YouTube videos. As soon as the video starts getting a lot of views, it accumulates. It has a feedback growth effect.

Some people, like Jeff Bezos, make more than $1,000,000,000 profit in a day because they've built up their beliefs, and they've confirmed those beliefs immeasurably with their actions. They've built robust, invincible automation infrastructures and an upward spiraling feedback loop.

A common misconception is when people think about creating a course and starting to build an audience, they think they need to design and build a full blown website: a blog, custom design, pictures, about page, social links, pop-ups, slide-ins, and so on. The truth is that you don't need any of these bells and whistles yet!

That's great news, especially if you're just getting started and don't even have a website yet.

Focus on the Pareto principle—20% of your actions will get you 80% of your results the fastest, and the rest will naturally fall into place with time and smart work.

The funny thing about human nature is that people naturally procrastinate the things that make the biggest positive changes the fastest, because they're generally the things furthest from our comfort zones.

You're going to be tempted to do anything other than the work you need to do to be successful. You're starting a brand new chapter in your life that has the potential to change everything. Some things are going to be challenging, pushing you outside of your comfort zone, and you're going to want to do anything other than the work.

The people who achieve success take full responsibility for themselves and their situations. You need to take full responsibility and understand that where you are in life right now is your own doing.

Getting Started

Paul Graham, the founder of Y Combinator, one of the most successful startup accelerators in the world, tells all of his founders to "do things that don't scale" when they're first getting started. That's the secret to how companies with tremendous growth "magically" take off.

Let's take Airbnb for example. Airbnb is now valued at $30+ billion. The Airbnb founders actually went door to door in New York City to recruit new users one by one. They even photographed their apartments themselves in the beginning.

The Airbnb founders also sold Obama and McCain-themed cereal when they were starting literally to stay alive and keep Airbnb afloat while it was making no money and no one believed in them. Think about that for a second.

If billionaires sold cereal to make it work and went door to door signing up people one at a time, taking pictures of apartments themselves one by one, you know you have to do whatever it takes.

Create your own cereal if you have to. Go door to door if you have to. My point is the billionaire mentality doesn't include a definition for giving up. There's only the next experiment that is bound to be successful!

To start getting your first traffic for your course, you'll do things differently than you will once you get those critical 1,000 followers. I want you to be aware that in the beginning, you will have to fight tooth and nail for every follower, every member of your group, every subscriber, and each and every email address.

Remember, the growth curve is not linear, it is exponential, but you have to reach the point where you receive that exponential payoff. Most people give up long before that point.

Think about trying to light a fire without matches or a lighter. You have to rub sticks together for hours until your arms feel like they're going to break. You need to blow on the embers delicately to try and spark them. You need to nurture it. It can take what feels like forever, but once you have the fire burning, it grows and roars, and you continue to add fuel to the fire!

What's Stopping You?

So, if everyone knows they need to be reaching out and finding their ideal customers at all costs at the beginning, then why aren't they doing it?

Well, there are TWO reasons...

Reason #1: Fear

When you actively seek out feedback, you'll likely run into opinions that create more work for you or might not be what you'd like to hear. People might surprise you with their answers. People might challenge your assumptions, meaning you may have to re-evaluate your ideas. However, that's how your ideas get better and more refined.

This might require a shift in your mindset. Negative feedback doesn't mean you or your course idea sucks. It means it's not positioned to fit the needs of the people you're reaching. It's critical you maintain objectivity and never rely on the feedback of any single person to dictate your actions.

Once you stop looking at critical feedback as rejections, you can start to use it to make the courses you offer much better.

Reason #2: The "It's Not Worth It" Attitude

This happens when people want to start a business, but when they have the chance to get their first customer, they think: "Eh, it's just one customer. It's not worth it." Either you want to build a business and you'll value each and every subscriber, or you just don't want to start a business at this scale. You have to nurture the fire before it starts to roar and burn brilliantly.

When I first started my movement, I would add every single person I talked to or who showed any sort of interest in me or my content to my Facebook groups. I worked with them individually, answering all of their questions, and fostering the family feeling.

I did that with literally HUNDREDS, if not thousands, of people. Even though I was only adding one person at a time, every one of those people had friends, or knew other Amazon sellers, or would eventually meet them. In today's day and age, word travels like wildfire on the internet!

You build your brand one person and one interaction at a time! Now I understand, when you build your list with things that don't scale, subscribers trickle in slowly at first. You'll get one subscriber a day, or maybe two subscribers. It doesn't seem like much, but going from one to two subscribers is literally DOUBLING your growth!

Even with ten subscribers, that is ten people who are interested in what you have to say, and what you have to sell, and with the right mentality, they can become life-long customers. So, foster those relationships, truly help people get the answers they need, treat every subscriber like they are family, and just watch the profound effect it has on your business.

Chapter 12
Shattering the Glass Ceiling:
How to Find Your First Customers

"Nothing attracts a crowd like a crowd."
— P.T. Barnum

Take some time to define your market and give them an avatar.

You need to be best friends with your customer avatar. What do they do? How do they spend their week? What do they do outside of work? Where do they get their news? How much money do they make? How do they feel about their job? What are their concerns about life? What aspects of their life or personality affect how you market your product to them?

If your ideal client is a certain type of business, can you start searching through Google right now and build a list of potential customers?

If you've chosen your niche as digital marketing for dentists, can you just go to Google and start searching for dentists? If you can, awesome. Now, you want to think, "Do these dentists match my avatar?"

SARAH AVATAR

OCCUPATION OR DESCRIPTIVE TITLE

- WHERE DO THEY LIVE?
- HOW OLD ARE THEY?
- WHAT IS THEIR LEVEL OF EDUCATION?
- WHAT HAVE THEY ACCOMPLISHED?

MEET SARAH.

TELL US A LITTLE ABOUT YOUR AVATAR. WHAT DO THEY DO? HOW DO THEY SPEND THEIR WEEK? WHAT DO THEY DO OUTSIDE OF WORK? WHERE DO THEY GET THEIR NEWS?

HOW MUCH DO THEY MAKE? HOW DO THEY FEEL ABOUT THEIR JOB? WHAT ARE THEIR CONCERNS IN LIFE? WHAT ASPECTS OF THEIR LIFE OR PERSONALITY AFFECT HOW YOU MARKET YOUR PRODUCT TO THEM?

TELL US ABOUT THEIR HISTORY. WHAT HAPPENED IN THE PAST THAT LED THEM UP TO THIS POINT? HOW DO THEY FEEL ABOUT WHAT HAPPENED IN THE PAST? PERHAPS A FORMER JOB, AN EXPERIENCE THEY HAD, OR A TRIP THAT THEY TOOK. WHAT ARE THEY CURRENTLY INTERESTED IN BECAUSE OF THIS EVENT?

WHAT IS THEIR FAMILY AND RELATIONSHIP STATUS? ARE THEY MARRIED? DIVORCED? SINGLE? DO THEY HAVE CHILDREN? HOW MANY? DOES ANYTHING ABOUT THEIR RELATIONSHIPS HAVE A BEARING ON HOW THEY MIGHT USE YOUR PRODUCT OR FIT IT INTO THEIR WEEK? DOES YOUR PRODUCT ADDRESS ANY OF THEIR CONCERNS THAT RELATE TO THEIR FAMILY?

WHAT IS IT ABOUT YOUR PRODUCT THAT MATTERS TO THIS PERSON? HOW DOES IT SOLVE A NEED, EASE A PAIN, OR MAKE THEM FEEL GOOD? HOW DOES IT BETTER THEIR LIFE?

WHAT SORT OF THOUGHTS SHOULD GO THROUGH THIS PERSON'S HEAD RIGHT BEFORE THEY DECIDE TO PURCHASE YOUR PRODUCTS? WHAT IS THE "FINAL STRAW" THAT MAKES THEM PULL THE TRIGGER?

Remember your momentum will be slow at first and will build exponentially. The compound interest you're earning by adding and interacting with your target audience one person at a time grows slowly until you reach the point of exponential return, when your audience explodes!

Finding Your Customer

Peter Thiel, the billionaire co-founder of PayPal, said that going from $0 to $1,000 per month is significantly harder than going from $1,000 to $10,000 per month, even though it is a much larger jump!

Why is that? It is because growth is not linear, it's exponential. Your daily actions build, grow, and stack. There is a breaking point where the compound interest you've been accumulating for those daily actions pays you back beyond your wildest dreams!

When people are interested in you, other people become interested in you just for the sole reason that other people are—it's just like walking down the street when you see a group of people looking up at something, it's human nature to look up also!

So, when you start to build momentum and a few people start noticing, all of a sudden, a few more do, and it builds exponentially!

If you have one person follow you (outside of friends and family), you instantly have more followers than 99% of people on Earth. You are creating content, and you are no longer just an observer like everyone else. You are a creator, and that is the only place you want to be!

Chapter 13
The Big Three

"Opportunity is missed by most people because it is
dressed in overalls and looks like work."
— Thomas Edison

In the next few chapters, you will learn how to start the most scalable, most important form of social media—YouTube. You will also learn to build a Facebook presence and control the platform where your tribe communicates, which will be your Facebook group, and finally, you will learn how to start building your email list.

You don't want to feel overloaded by focusing on every social media platform. When I first started, I was posting on Reddit, Pinterest, Twitter, basically ALL social media, and it was taking so much time. I was killing myself, but I started to track where all my course sales and best customers were actually coming from. I found out of every 100 sales, most were coming from YouTube, my Facebook group, and my email list. Some were also coming from Instagram, LinkedIn, and other social media, but it was less than 3%. That means that 97% of my sales came from three places, the Big 3: YouTube, my Facebook group, and Email.

The fatal mistake is to try to release content every day across all platforms. This leads to guaranteed failure because all of your energy will be expended on social media equally when there are the Big 3 you should be focusing on.

ROI and Relativity

It's critical to understand that, as an entrepreneur, there are two sides to focus. There is the side where you need to decide what to focus on, and there is the side where you need to decide what NOT to focus on.

Most people think you should use Instagram because everyone is using Instagram and it's the new cool thing. However, if I compare Instagram, which would take time to learn and master and create content for, and compare it to other activities I could use that same time and mental energy for, such as YouTube or building my Facebook group, the relative return is much lower.

The highest ROI is through your Facebook group or creating proven YouTube content. So, using Instagram would decrease your overall results because it would distract you from those things you know to be the highest ROI activities since your mental energy is finite. When you do one thing it takes away from another, remember that!

When you're getting started, it's vital for you as an entrepreneur to understand the idea of energy distribution and mental fatigue. If you focus on Instagram, it takes away from a proven strategy to get closer to your goals. You must remain focused in the face of distraction.

Just focus on YouTube, your Facebook group, and your email list at the start. The rest of your time and effort will be spent adding value and creating content for your following, learning, building proof of concept through gathering emails and having people show interest in what you have to say via subscribing to your YouTube, joining your Facebook groups, and creating success stories and testimonials.

Chapter 14

Owning the Communication
Platform: Your Facebook Group

Communication Is Key

F acebook groups are incredibly important. Owning the
community where people in your niche communicate gives
you a massive advantage. Keeping it a clean, spam free,
positive environment is critical for success.

Focus on people. You can get valuable feedback from them about
what they really want, what their pain is, how you can add value, and
how you can personally help related to your specific niche.

Getting your customers into different communication mediums,
such as your Facebook group, subscribed to your YouTube channel,
or on your email list is the single most critical factor to success.

If you can't communicate with your customers, you have nothing!

There are a lot of people who've gone viral and built up massive
interest just to disappear. This happens because they don't capture
that attention currency into communication mediums; they don't get
email addresses, YouTube subscribers, or Facebook Group members.

If you can't communicate with your customers, if you don't have
OPEN mediums of communication, you have nothing! You must
add value and help people for free to grow your followership, but you

also must incentivize them to give you their email, join your Facebook group, and subscribe to you on YouTube, so when you are ready to sell your course or make some kind of offer, you have a way to reach them at the click of a button.

These are the three MOST important forms of communication to be able to reach your customers most efficiently—and understanding each in depth is vital for creating your movement the most efficient way.

Your Public Facebook Group (The Community)

Create a Facebook group that is ultra-relevant to your specific niche. If you're making a course on how to build a real estate empire with Airbnb, you would want to make your Facebook group about that and call it "BnB Mastery."

I like to post at least five helpful things into the Facebook group immediately when I create it, so it's not empty. This can be other people's content you find interesting and related to your niche; it's fine to use as long as you credit them! Populate at least a basic announcement, description, and cover photo.

Look at one of my groups as an example: "Digital Course Secrets!"

Which by the way if you haven't already joined, you should; it's an unbelievable advantage having a group of like-minded people to learn with!

Don't try to reinvent the wheel, just simply copy and paste my announcement post and change the links to your own social media. As your business grows, and you create your cheatsheet and course, you'll update the links as you go.

You can also "Ask a Question" to new members asking for their email address in exchange for your lead magnet, which you will create later on. If you want an example, join one of my groups to see how I do it (just head to Facebook and search "Digital Course Secrets" under groups!). I suggest only asking for their email at first, don't ask three questions (which I do) until you have a group that people can't live without!

I also like to choose a URL that makes sense and is close to what I name the group; you can do this in your settings. If you don't know how, use the GIN mentality and GOOGLE IT NOW!

Your Private Facebook Group

I also created a private version of my public Facebook group. So if I called my public group "Digital Course Secrets," I would call my private group "Digital Course Secrets (Private Family Group)."

This is the group you will add your students to once they join your course. This is also the group you can add your Beta testers to, if you choose to go that route to validate your Proof of Concept, which I will explain later on.

At first, you will help everyone in your public and private group, but as your group grows in size, you'll start to focus on the people who invest in your course and help them all one-on-one!

Be extremely active in your private Facebook group, even if you only have one person in your group to start. If they have a question, answer it and post content frequently.

How to Get Your First Facebook Group Members

If you use just one unscalable strategy to start, this is the strategy I want you to use. But it's also one of the hardest to do.

First, you need to find five people to do FREE consultations with—the purpose will be to learn the real pain your market feels concerning your niche topic.

There are two types of consultations: free 15-minute consultations and paid consultations. With the 15-minute consultation you're gathering valuable data about your potential buyers and their common pain. Paid consultations, which we will **discuss** in later chapters, help you establish that your course idea is something people would actually pay for.

If you already have an email list with 100 or more subscribers, it's easy. Just send a message to your list and offer a free 15-minute consultation.

If you don't have any subscribers or members on your email list, join relevant Facebook groups. If you're creating an Amazon course, go and join all the large active Amazon groups by searching Amazon FBA into the Facebook search bar and filtering for groups. If you're making a photography course, join all the active photography groups.

Once you're a member of the group, reach out to the owner BEFORE you share your free thing and ask if you can post it for free value. This is generally what I've found to be the best way to do things. They might not answer, but it's better etiquette to do so!

Just post value, and when people comment, answer their comments, and at the end of your comments, say, "Feel free to message me if you have any more questions!"

You could make a post on the top 10 ways to lose weight for summer, or the 5 best free SEO tools, or the top 3 Amazon FBA product research tips. It doesn't matter, as long as it is what you feel is most valuable and what your market most desires!

You can see what your market most desires in a number of ways, see what the most popular YouTube videos on your subject are about, see what books are about, see what people say to you in your free consultations from people you find in relevant Facebook groups, etc.

Just remember to post pure value; don't try to drive anyone to any of your own stuff!

This is actually an important step because you don't want to lose momentum and be banned from the large groups by blatantly promoting your own stuff with links.

Plus, it's just good form.

Think of it like this: inside someone's group, it's like you're in the owner's house. They have to maintain it and keep it free of spam, just as you eventually will for your group, so they make the rules.

The people you speak with can become your beta testers, which we will discuss later.

Many people will message you if your post adds massive value, and doesn't get removed (because you've reached out to the group owner, and are NOT linking to your content).

To the people who end up messaging you to thank you or to ask for additional help, I would respond with something like this:

"Hey [NAME],

It's great you're interested in [YOUR NICHE], I'm actually forming a beta group where I'm going to be helping people with [YOUR NICHE] completely for free. If you're interested, let me know, and I'll get you added!"

Then ask for their email to add them, and you will have your first email, which is a massive step!

What's the Process?

1. Post 3-5 pieces of content on your Facebook profile (or the largest, most active communities where your potential customers congregate) to prove you're real and in your niche.

2. Block out one hour every day on your calendar to dedicate to this method.

3. Search for relevant Facebook groups related to your niche, join them and observe.

4. Start adding 40 active contributing group members from those relevant groups per day as Facebook friends and

message them (no more than 40 or Facebook could limit you).

5. Ask what they're struggling with and if you could help. Advance the conversation toward a 15-minute phone chat to learn more about what they're struggling with exactly (this information becomes very valuable - as you can gather info about your market's pain straight from the market itself!).

6. Post valuable content and personal updates on your Facebook profile daily and inside your Facebook group! You want to make it clear in your own personal Facebook what you do, so add a sentence detailing what you help people do! When you make posts and message people, they will naturally view your profile to see what you're about, so you want to present a clear, clean professional image!

Utilizing the Group

As you join these groups, Facebook should display "groups that are similar to this." Look at the suggestions and join those groups too. When you get inside the different groups, try to identify the "Influencers."

These are group members who are respected in the group and typically know what they're talking about and have experience. Find these people, look at the pages and groups they're in by viewing their profile, and then join those groups, too. You can also find suggested groups in the sidebar when you join, and this will give you ideas of more related groups to join!

Now that you're in these Facebook groups, take some time to observe what goes on inside them. What are people saying? What are the common posts, comments, arguments, ambitions, goals, problems, pains, etc.?

Observe, take notes, and get ideas for your ads, content posts, videos, landing page, and even your sales calls and offer itself. You want to start small, simple, and organic. Start by joining Facebook groups, posting content on your Facebook and LinkedIn profiles, growing your friend and connection lists, direct messaging, building relationships, setting up free consulting calls to learn about what they're struggling with and how you can help, and gathering information about what the real pain and desires are in your niche from real people.

Facebook is infinitely more important than LinkedIn. I only even mention LinkedIn because, for some business-to-business course topics, it's more relevant. If you're creating a course on how to start an accounting firm or something similar, then LinkedIn becomes much more relevant. It's just another easy lead gen technique, but Facebook should get 90% of your attention in most cases!

You want to start with organic means of lead generation because it can be deployed immediately and because it's free. You can also iterate and test rapidly to get your message refined and get your first few clients.

In the beginning when you're just getting started in business, you have a lot of time and not a lot of money, so use your time. Then once you start making money, you start to have less time—the magic of finite energy, cause and effect.

Adding Group Members As Friends (Building Your Initial Following)

Remember, you are not like most people. When I first started making courses, I didn't use paid advertisements because I thought to myself, "I would never click a Facebook ad and buy a course…" but just because I wouldn't, does not mean other people won't! They do every single day by the thousands!

I'm going to repeat this again because it is CRITICAL to understand: just because you wouldn't click a Facebook ad and buy a course, or you wouldn't like someone messaging you offering free consulting, does NOT mean other people are the same.

This is the same thing with adding people as friends, sending them messages, and adding them to your group. Most people actually find it awesome that people want to help them, even if you don't!

With those who are annoyed by it, simply apologize and move on, no harm done. You can be someone who feels uncomfortable about adding people as friends and to your groups and enjoy your cubicle, or you can expand your comfort zone and flourish; it really is as simple as that!

To add people as friends, look at the recent posts and comments in the relevant Facebook groups, and then click on the person's name to see their profile and determine whether they're a good fit for your services. If you think they're a good fit, add them as a friend.

I generally target people who are asking intelligent questions or seem like beginners in need of some guidance. This means they want to learn, are comfortable learning via Facebook, and are active in the group, meaning they will probably be active in your group!

Another way to find members and add them as friends is to click the "Members" link within the group. This will show you all the group members. Scroll through them and look at their profiles to determine whether they're a good fit. If they are, add them as friends.

WARNING: Facebook will "limit" your account and remove your ability to add new friends if you try to add more than ~40 per day. Make sure you never add more than 40 people every 24 hours. Treat this as a daily exercise that will flourish over time. It's a marathon, not a sprint.

If you're getting less than a 50% response rate, this means your profile isn't appealing to your niche, so you need to work on it and make it more appealing. If you're selling to a professional crowd, try a suit pic for your profile picture, and upgrade your cover photo. You can get ideas from the top influencers in your niche!

When initially reaching out to active group members you're adding, you could send a message that says something like:

> "I saw you're an [ACCOUNTANT] and I wanted to reach out.
> I'm [YOUR NAME] and I help [ACCOUNTANTS] to [GET MORE CLIENTS].
> I was wondering if I might be able to add value to you (completely for free of course!)"

When you direct message Facebook friends, roughly 50% of the people you message will reply to you. So, if you add 40 new friends a day, 20 will accept and read your messages. If you message all 20, roughly 50% of those people will reply, and from those 10 who do reply, you can advance the conversation toward a free consultation to learn more. Once you start to get some people entering your group, you want to encourage them to post when they have success!

Sometimes if people tell me on Facebook they got a client or helped someone lose weight, or find a relationship, but they don't post about it because they're shy or busy, I'll just take a screenshot of their message to me. Then I'll post it in the Facebook group and congratulate them. This is not bragging. It is motivation for your other members to get into gear, so they can get that recognition of success! That is also how you build a strong community!

Think of cool, innovative ways to share what results people are getting and put it in the group. The key here is you want to show people that others are getting results with your program because they are looking for feedback. People are constantly trying to evaluate what the best use of their time is. They want to know:

"Is this the best use of my time to get me from [PAIN] to [PLEASURE]?"

Your job is basically to do two things, document, and observe. You're trying to identify common confusion points and problem points. Once you notice an obvious pattern where everybody gets confused or stuck at a particular part of the training, write it down so you can make it extremely clear in your course! If you want to, add a supplementary training to the portal to solve it.

Now, a lot of you will probably think, "Well, how do I know if it's an obvious pattern?" It'll be blatantly obvious. You only want to build an extra thing, and you only know it's a problem when it's blatant. Lots of people are stumbling in a particular spot, and it's an obvious trend.

If one person is stumbling, it doesn't mean it's a problem. Even if a few people are stumbling, it doesn't mean it's a problem. Only if it's happening again and again, so often that it obviously requires additional clarity. To make it clearer, sometimes the best thing to do is add examples or give them step-by-step instructions, tutorials, and share your screen and literally walk them through it.

Fostering Engagement

 Kevin David shared a link.

⚙ Admin · Published by Eugene Sarino [?] · 15 December at 09:00

🔥 Welcome to the Amazon Ninja Family!

😎 Let me Know the #1 Thing You Want to Learn About Amazon Below!

👉 Click HERE to Join the Top 1% Amazon Training:
http://bit.ly/FreeAmznTraining

Shawn
Natalie
Nancy
Matt
Candace
Austin
León
Kip
Tracey
Tranal
Jomirah
Lilly
Yury
Ronald
Sami
Bob
Kris
Peter
Jerry
Adel
Faheem
Manea
Alise
Arturo
Sukru
Brooke
Tara
Lindsey
Najm
Jake

As people join your group, you want to tag them all. This makes your new members feel special and increases engagement!

I use a virtual assistant to do this. Just add them as a moderator and teach them how to tag new members in a daily post asking them to introduce themselves. Some of my smartest, most loyal, and grateful employees I've found in this manner, and they still work for me full time.

When tagged, members get a notification from you, which gets them into the habit of using the group. This is a critical step most people forget!

This is incredibly important because it helps with your EdgeRank, the algorithm Facebook uses to determine what articles will be displayed in a user's News Feed. This will make your Facebook group appear higher in natural search results. For example, if someone typed "Fitness Group," if you have the most engagement, you will appear first and get many more organic joins!

You can also use a link to your lead magnet or webinar (once you create it if you have a high-ticket product) to capture emails and get them further into your ecosystem. Remember, you always want to make it as easy as possible for your students and followers to give you their email address.

Once your group reaches 500 members, you want to go live, dropping value bombs at least once per month with prepared topics but also with live Q and A broadcasts on YouTube and FB! Interaction is key to fostering a family feeling and community!

Lastly, you want to set up your cover photo for your Facebook Group and Facebook page. You can use my group cover photos as an example, "FBA Ninjas," or the most popular group in your niche!

Chapter 15
Drawing Them In:
How to Get More Email Addresses

Lead Magnets

One of your most valuable assets is your email list. The best way to build your email list is with a lead magnet. A lead magnet is something of super high value you give away for free in exchange for people's emails.

You need to create your lead magnet at this stage, related to your course, based on successful examples of those already in your niche. Lead magnets should NEVER be vague. They must offer an ultra-specific solution to an ultra-specific market.

This is the #1 problem with most lead magnets—they simply aren't specific enough.

A lead magnet is anything IRRESISTIBLE to your perfect customer or your target market. If you were making a niche about weight loss, you could use "Top 10 Foods to Avoid When You're Trying to Lose Weight!" Or with a course on Amazon, it could be "10,000 BEST Selling Products on Amazon!"

The more specific you make it from a targeting perspective, the more likely someone is to really want it. This goes back to our research phase in Part 1. If everyone has the same question about your niche, you want to make a cheatsheet answering that question in detail.

A great tactic to use is looking at the major players in your niche, download all of their cheatsheets, see what you like and what you don't, and make yours better!

Look at their title. How are they attracting attention? How do they organize their content? What is their eventual CTA or Call to Action at the end? Is it to subscribe to them on YouTube? Follow their Instagram? Do they have an embedded link to their course?

You want your cheatsheet to give whoever reads it some quick wins and results. If you can do this and embed a link directly to your Facebook group, your order page, or to purchase something from you, you will WIN!

Quick wins make your customers happy and feel progress, and leave your audience wanting more, leading them to buy from you.

It's very important to remember that you should never reinvent the wheel. There's no point. Whenever I need to build an email campaign, make a new cheatsheet or video, I look at what is out there and think about how I could make it way, way better. The sooner you get into this mindset, the easier all of this will become for you.

Need a new email campaign? Go subscribe to the best email marketers in the world and use their emails as inspiration. Need some new YouTube topics? Search general keywords in your niche, see what has the most views, and improve it.

People who spend a month on an email campaign lose. People who spend three days on an email campaign by looking at the best email marketers and then using their emails as inspiration win.

Never copy, that's just not right. However, using things as inspiration is perfectly fine. You would be foolish not to!

People dedicate their lives to YouTube or learning email marketing or Facebook; they are experts. Not leveraging their dedication and mastery would be extremely stupid. Again, never directly copy, but using them as inspiration is perfectly fine.

You can create any number of things as your lead magnet like a Cheatsheet, Mini-Course, Checklist, eBook, Template, Script, Swipe Files, or How to Guides.

To see countless examples of any of these, simply Google search "Amazon Cheatsheet" or "How to talk to women script" or "How to get abs checklist" for whatever your specific niche is. Take what is working and add your own unique creativity to it.

The Power of Free Content

Your lead magnets will be used to start collecting emails, building your Facebook groups, and building rapport by giving more free content to your tribe.

You'll also use your cheatsheets to build your email lists once we get into paid advertising down the line, but it's an incredibly important step and will make you a ton of money!

Let's look at how this works. At first, you have no following. Think of your customers as stumbling around in Times Square with a million advertisements around them. You have to attract their attention somehow and be able to keep an open conversation with them via communication mediums. The best way to do that is through free value in the form of cheatsheets, YouTube videos, and one-on-ones.

Most people do it wrong and try to charge for everything. Give away everything for free at first, and you'll make 100x more than if you try to charge up front!

I always include my cheatsheet links inside my Facebook groups in the pinned post and description, and say where people can get them in my YouTube videos. For example, you'd say, "If you want to download the 'Top 50 Amazon products to sell in 2019', click the link in the description and you'll be taken to our Facebook group where you can get one-on-one help." The link to the cheatsheet will be in the pinned post and the description!

This means you get people into Facebook groups and you get their emails. The more points of contact you have with people, the better this works.

I hope you're starting to get just how powerful this gets and the critical importance of getting people into multiple forms of communication as soon as possible!

Chapter 16

Funnels Are the Future

A Wise Investment

F unnels are the new website. A sales funnel is a series of steps or web pages used to guide the user toward taking an action or buying a product or service. Funnels are where you will send your YouTube viewers, Facebook group members to start collecting emails. Later on, you'll use funnels to sell your course! ClickFunnels is the infrastructure upon which the backbone of my digital empire is built.

ClickFunnels is an amazing sales funnel builder for entrepreneurs. For an exclusive free trial to ClickFunnels visit: www.officialkevindavid.com/clickfunnels

You've probably heard people say it takes money to make money, which is true—most businesses require a ton of upfront capital in the form of buying products or brick and mortar businesses that require office buildings or rent, but creating a course requires very few upfront costs. This book is dedicated to sparing you every possible expense, so know that when I do mention something, it is because it is a necessity.

Your Domain

ClickFunnels is indescribably worth the money, so sign up for your free trial from the link I mentioned. Once you've started your free trial at ClickFunnels, you want to claim your free Domain or URL.

My domain is www.officialkevindavid.com. Now, you're going to claim yours!

You should have chosen your personal brand, or brand name in Part 1 (again I recommend using your name or some simplified version of it—I regret using THATLifestyleNinja at first, and it was a pain to switch it everywhere), and now it is time to claim your domain inside ClickFunnels using that same name.

If your name is taken, you can add "official" before it, or "inc", or "the", or "ask", or anything you want; it's yours!

Everyone gets one free domain inside ClickFunnels. To learn how and any/all of the technical portions of the book, head over to www.digitalcoursesecrets.com/go.

The Email Autoresponder I Recommend is ActiveCampaign

An email autoresponder allows you to send multiple emails to many different people at once. I suffered for months with email autoresponders trying to find the most reliable, best solution, and it honestly isn't even close. Learn the best from the start. With ActiveCampaign, you can share entire email automations with the click of a button that used to take months to create. It's incredible software!

To sign up for ActiveCampaign with our exclusive offer, go to the following URL:

www.officialkevindavid.com/activecampaign

Once you sign up for your ActiveCampaign plan, you need to integrate and link your ActiveCampaign account to your ClickFunnels account. Once you've integrated them, you're one step closer to a million dollar course ecosystem!

Funnels are the Future

In the old business model, you would hand out a business card or brochure or send newsletters, hoping someone stumbles across your ad and follows up. In the new business model, your product is at their fingertips and immediately benefits your customer. You give them something of value, and they can learn something right away. They think, "Wow, that worked. I want more of it." In the new business, people are expecting to receive the benefits immediately, rather than just hear about them.

Chapter 17

The Infinite Free Traffic Monster: YouTube

I want you to say the following out loud, so it's CRYSTAL CLEAR:

"The key to making a successful course and creating a movement is consistently creating YOUTUBE CONTENT. I understand the HARDEST PART is getting my first 1,000 Subscribers. Being consistent on YouTube is the single most important thing I can POSSIBLY do to be successful with my course."

You only have to do the work once. Then you can scale the proper way, capture people's emails, and get them into your Facebook group, and you won't make all of the mistakes I made. Do it right the FIRST TIME!

Think about it like this, you create a YouTube video, you do all this work, get your camera, and let's say 1,000 people end up watching it. Pretty great, right?

Out of those 1,000 people, maybe 100 of them would be interested enough to give you their email for a cheatsheet or join your Facebook group.

Out of those 100 people, maybe 10 would read an email you sent a month afterward and would buy your course for $997.

If you don't have your lead magnet and Facebook group readily accessible, you could have lost $10,000!

With YouTube, it can be difficult to get momentum, which is why most people give up. Most people will make a few videos, get a few views, not get that instant gratification we have become so accustomed to, and quit.

The person who creates proven YouTube content consistently and strategically (two videos per week—remaking already popular video topics) for 90 days will be successful. However, most people will give up before they hit the exponential growth curve.

For example, have you ever followed a YouTuber since they started out and it took them a year to grow from 0-5,000 subscribers?

And then suddenly, in a month, they've gone from 5,000 to 50,000?

This is the exponential growth model, and it's very real on YouTube, in business, and life. Those who lay the groundwork and are consistent stay in the game long enough to reap the benefits of the exponential growth curve and compound interest for their incremental actions!

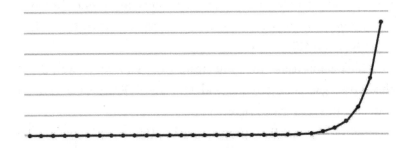

YouTube is also the SINGLE BIGGEST REASON I've grown my business from 0-8 figures in such a short time and is the number one most important thing I do, without question!

My Main CTA (Call to Action)

My CTA is to get people to subscribe because it is the most important thing to me. I follow it up with my FREE webinar on how to Sell on Amazon, which has converted the most course sales by far for me.

In this video, I discuss a lead magnet I put together called the Ninja Magic Words that people need to give their emails to get!

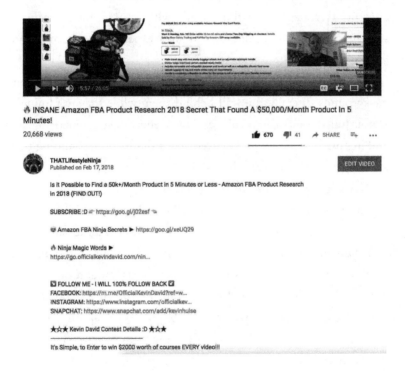

The hardest part of this process is getting started. Your first 1,000 subscribers will be the hardest, but remember that anything worth something is never easy.

What I learned about YouTube is that if you create quality content people will view it for years. I have a video I made over a year ago that still gets 1,000 views per day. Talk about unlimited free traffic!

There is nothing else on Earth that allows you to target so many interested people completely for free!

If you don't know what type of content to make literally search for content related to your niche on YouTube, see what is most popular and getting the most views, and then create similar content!

Remember, YouTube PROVES what the majority of people are interested in through views—you do not WANT TO REINVENT the wheel. Simply add your own spin or twist on already successful content, recreate similar thumbnails with you in them, recreate similar titles, and add your own unique experiences, passion, and energy!

Look for people in your niche, and see if you like their backgrounds (literally the wall behind them while they're filming). People judge your video quality and the scenery in your video quickly and intensely. You will grow faster than I did by understanding this and implementing it from the start!

Never allow yourself to feel overwhelmed. It is the poison to success! One of the most popular YouTubers in the world, Mr. Beast, made videos for 5 YEARS consistently and got next to no return. All of a sudden, he absolutely exploded and became one of the highest earning YouTubers in the world making over 1 million dollars per month! With the strategies I've laid out for you in this book, you won't have to wait anywhere near 5 years to reap the rewards YouTube has to offer - the trick is to remain consistent while other people give up!

Chapter 18

Invincible Omnipotent Impact: Your Following

Your following is your best possible chance to make the largest positive impact on the most people and is the easiest way to make money on the planet.

Every person who gives you their email, subscribes to you on YouTube, or follows you on any MEDIUM of communication is one more potential buyer. You have their attention. If you're consistently creating valuable content, you're building rapport!

You never have to worry about money again when you have a following because you can simply send an email, make a Facebook post, or a YouTube video and make sales.

Want to make another course or some software? Promote it to your following and watch it be instantly successful. Want to promote other people's software and get huge affiliate commissions? Do it!

Having a large following, especially one you've created success for, is the most valuable thing on Earth. It exponentiates money-making on a grander scale than most people expect!

Normally, you only have the power of one, which is yourself. Even if you work extremely hard you're just one person, but the reason I refer to attention as a "currency" is because it truly is.

When you have people's attention, you can create wealth that is very, very difficult to do otherwise and at speeds that are difficult to understand until you've experienced them.

If I want to make $100,000 in a day, I can send an email to my list. Even if everyone just gave 1 dollar, or 1 in a thousand people gives a thousand dollars, it works because there are hundred of thousands of people on it. I send an email, make $100 grand. Done.

When you add value to your customers, they refer you to other people. You start to grow all these different lists, and this builds your following over time. After a year or two, You'll look back and discover there are 100,000 people you can contact and upsell.

The most important thing to understand is you have to capture people into your mediums (or following). Add as many people as you can to your Facebook Group, get as many YouTube followers as possible, and get as many email addresses as you can.

Email is one of the most important because Instagram or Facebook can always disable your account, but your emails are yours forever. You can just switch email providers if something ever happened!

Any time you sell something or promote something, you have people who are interested in what you have to say and ready to buy.

It is such a powerful thing being able to reach people with the click of a button and watch your bank account fill with money WHILE (more importantly) helping people.

The way you do all of that is by adding massive amounts of value for free. Create communities, give people value and happiness, and you'll create a movement faster than you can imagine. When you focus on giving value and improving the lives of others, your life has a funny way of improving as well!

Something else to keep in mind is that as you build a following, or your tribe, you can make money in infinite ways. I have friends who charge $25,000 to spend the weekend at their house to learn one-on-one. I have friends who offer done-for-you copywriting or marketing solutions and charge thousands. I have friends who do nothing but promote affiliate offers to their followings and make millions.

Even if only one person watches your YouTube video, that is one more follower than 99% of the world.

Remember, time is the universal constant. Time still passes whether or not you're building your following, so after a month you have maybe a hundred followers, and your competitors have none. That means whenever you release something, you have one hundred people instantly interested in buying it!

A CULT-ure of Success

You're not just teaching people about Facebook ads, funnels, or whatever you teach in your niche. You're teaching an entire way of living.

Success is a way of thinking. It's a way of behaving. It's an identity. It involves changes in your routine, your day's structure. It requires you to be disciplined. It requires you to work hard. Sometimes, it requires shifts in thinking.

I like to cement this with imagery; a picture speaks a thousand words. That is why using a vision board can help.

Think about the person you most admire, the person with the life most similar to what you want. Maybe it means you're rich or famous, or maybe it means you're a meditating monk at one with your spirituality. It doesn't matter what it is, but you want to define it so you can focus on it every single day and move closer toward it.

For me, it was Elon Musk. When I first started this journey, I printed out a picture of his face and literally put it on my wall right next to my computer. I know it sounds silly, but every time I felt like giving up, I looked at him and I asked myself, "Do I want to be average, or do I want to be extraordinary?" Sometimes you're going to have a bad day, and you need mental anchor points to bring you back into it.

The NEM Top 3 (Nothing Else Matters)

You'll be tempted to do anything other than these 3 things:

1. Recreate two passionate, proven YouTube videos weekly on your course topic.
2. Add 40 targeted people per day as friends on Facebook and message them.
3. Nurture and build your Facebook group with daily content and help every single member one-on-one every day.

I tell my students to focus on these three things. This one sheet of paper has probably created more results than anything else I've ever done.

When you look at your NEM Top 3, read them out loud to yourself as often as you can, and then imagine you have already achieved your goals and your vision.

Make the image in your mind detailed and colorful, experience the vision fully and let the positive emotions run through your body again and again.

Adopting the ODAAT (ONE DAY AT A TIME) Mentality

What you're going to do in the short span of this book takes most people years if not decades to do. The people who will succeed are those who approach this with the one day at a time mentality (ODAAT).

Maybe one day you get some graphics made for your YouTube channel, and one day you set up your Facebook group and get your cover photo done, then a few days later, you get your lead magnet set up using our template (available at www.digitalcoursesecrets.com/go).

The point is don't have any zero days, always be chipping away. Do something, even if it's just answering one comment in your Facebook group.

Your emotions will scream, you will leave your comfort zone, you will feel fear, discomfort, pain. Understand that it's a completely normal reaction when you're working towards creating your dream life.

Don't think these emotions mean you should stop. If anything, they mean you should double down, go harder. They mean you're going after the right thing.

But you must stick to what is taught. It may not feel like it's working at first, but after a few days or a few weeks of discipline, it becomes habit. When you have hard-working habits making incremental impact consistently over time, all of a sudden, everything changes.

You want to face the fear head on, stare it in the eyes, and defeat it. Once you've done it, do it again and again and again. You want to develop extreme self-discipline to do what needs to be done every day. If you do that, you'll stick to the plan. If you stick to the plan, you'll get the result.

> *"The most dangerous distractions are the ones you love,*
> *but that don't love you back."*
> — Warren Buffett

This means Instagram, Snapchat, Reddit, Netflix, etc. Every time you're using these things, you're making the founders of those apps rich, but you're keeping yourself from your dreams.

When I first began as an entrepreneur, I couldn't see the reward right away. I let myself fall into the instant gratification spiral that society has normalized in today's day and age.

I was doing a lot of hard work. I was reading books, and blogs, and taking a bunch of action, but I wasn't seeing any results. A few months later, though, BOOM, all of a sudden, I remember thinking where is all this money pouring in from, how did this just come out of the blue?

That is when I realized I was reaping the benefits of the compound interest I had been accumulating over the past months by taking massive daily action. My growth curve started to look exponential rather than linear because that is simply how it works if you're working towards the right thing.

Steven Covey has a quote I love that says, "If the ladder is not leaning against the right wall, every step we take just gets us to the wrong place faster."

If the ladder is leaning against the RIGHT wall, which is creating a digital course movement, then each incremental daily action takes us closer to collecting the exponential compound interest.

Creating your digital course movement is truly the platinum link in business. If you want to create the largest, most meaningful empire in the shortest period, then get rid of distractions, focus on the blueprint, trust the process, and do the work every single day.

📖 Part 2 Summary

- You learned about how to become the attractive character your followers will want to follow and learn from.
- You learned about becoming the creator and the three types of course creators.
- You learned about the critical importance of getting your viewers and audience into communication mediums like your Public and Private Facebook groups, email list, and YouTube.
- You learned about the importance of offering free 15-minute consultations to people in relevant Facebook groups who need your help to better understand your particular market's pain and desires.
- You learned about how to find relevant targeted people in your niche, and how to add them as friends, open conversations, and get them into your Facebook group.
- You learned the importance of hiring a virtual assistant as soon as you can possibly start using one.
- You learned how to create your cheatsheet by looking at popular examples.
- You learned about the critical importance of consistency on YouTube.

✅ Part 2 Checklist

- Have you defined your attractive character and made sure your offer is future-based and described as a brand new opportunity? What is it?

- Have you chosen which type of course creator you'll become? Which is it?
- Have you created your public + private Facebook group?
- Have you offered at least 10 free 15-minute consultations to people from relevant Facebook groups, your YouTube videos, and your email list to learn their main questions? Have you helped them for free?
- Have you added at least 40 targeted/relevant people as friends on Facebook today, messaged them, and added them to your new public Facebook group?
- Have you downloaded and updated your lead magnet (ClickFunnels' landing page) to have your own images and ad copy, and tested that it works how you want it to?
- Have you made your first perfect YouTube video, optimized your YouTube channel with your intro, cover art, and end screen?

For even more resources to help you get your course out to the world, including:

- In-depth Clickfunnels support
- Example cheatsheets you can copy and change
- Example YouTube videos
- Example social media photos
- Access to my private Facebook group for support and accountability

Go to www.digitalcoursesecrets.com/go/

Part 3
Validating Your Course Idea with Real-World Data

Chapter 19
Validating Your Niche

"Every battle is won before it is fought."
— Sun Tzu

In the far east, the Chinese bamboo tree takes five years to sprout. Gardeners have to water and fertilize the ground where it is planted every day, but the tree doesn't break through the ground until the fifth year. However, once it breaks through the ground, within five weeks, it grows 90 feet tall. Now the question is, does it grow 90 feet tall in five weeks or five years?

The answer is obvious. It grows 90 feet tall in five years. At any time, had that person stopped watering, nurturing, and fertilizing that dream, that bamboo tree would've died in the ground.

This is a perfect real-world illustration of the effect of compound interest. Watering and nurturing the Bamboo tree for 5 years with nothing to show for it, then in 5 short weeks it grows to 90 feet tall!

This is why it's so important to KNOW you're working toward the right path!

Thinking your course idea sounds like a good idea, asking a few friends if they think it's a good idea, and then pushing forward full force with no market feedback or quantitative data is a catastrophic mistake.

Another critical mistake is trying to make your first idea, or idea you've always had for a course, try to fit when the data is against it.

Let's say one of my imaginary students named David wanted to create a course and chose the topic of underwater basket weaving. It doesn't really fall into the three evergreen topics, but it is his passion, so he went with it.

He did his research. He found a few videos on YouTube with under 1,000 views from years ago and not much activity on Facebook, but he still really liked the idea.

He tried to find people interested in underwater basket weaving. One of his friends, Beth, responded to a personal Facebook status he posted, offering his underwater basket weaving consultation.

He set up a free 15-minute call with Beth to sell the idea of a 60-minute paid consultation or done-for-you solution where David would consult one-on-one with Beth on how to be a first-class underwater basket weaver.

Beth, of course, declines, because no one is willing to pay for underwater basket weaving training. Unfortunately, she was the only interested party David could find.

This is obviously a ridiculous example, but similar things happen every day!

After doing due diligence, if you find there are no other courses on the niche, or communities on Facebook, or videos on YouTube, then do NOT do it—period.

Consultation versus Done-for-You

When you're first starting out and trying to get proof of concept, often times people will be more interested in a done-for-you solution than a paid consultation.

An example of a paid consultation for Amazon would be

reviewing someone's paid PPC campaigns and making suggestions or updates while trying to increase their profitability.

An example of a done-for-you solution for Amazon would be setting up someone's product listing, fully optimized from scratch, so they don't even have to touch it!

To establish proof of concept most efficiently, you need to first understand your market. You can make educated guesses about what people want, but until you talk to your market, you will never know for sure.

You want to ask all the people you've made contact with one question:

"What is your number 1 question about... [COURSE TOPIC]?"

This does a number of things, including helping you know exactly what free content to release on YouTube and what to release later in your Facebook group.

Chapter 20

Seeking Your Question Pattern

Guiding Questions

For YouTube, you will want to rely heavily on what is already working/popular because doing so drastically increases your sample size. If you talk to ten people, and they all say similar things, that's great, but YouTube has tens of thousands of views and shows you what the market is most interested in by the number of views on specific video topics.

YouTube is a *majority opinion aggregator*, so you need to keep in mind that if you have a small sample size, you can get mixed signals. Always trust YouTube and Google data if there are contradictions, as their data is collected on a much larger scale.

You want to be sure about the following:

1. Are you providing a new opportunity?
2. Are people irrationally passionate about it (do they have their own vocab—"autoresponder" is digital marketers' jargon)?
3. Are there forums, groups, podcasts, YouTube channels, and live events?

4. Are there pre-existing, successful experts in the space, and are people willing and able to spend money to learn more about it? Remember, competition is a good thing!

Those aggregated top answers will also guide you while writing your sales bullets when it comes time to create your sales page. Remember, everything is sequential and connected!

Objection Handling

Whatever your niche is, people have questions about it. Often, the majority of people have the same questions. Knowing the answers to those questions and alleviating their worries before they even potentially know they have them is a powerful sales tactic.

It's called Objection Handling, and it's one of the most powerful ways to make sales. If people are interested but all share the same concerns, if you preemptively shatter those worries and objections, you're going to make 100x more sales!

The following are the most common questions about getting started on Amazon. I learned these by asking the market with free consultations for ten people and reviewing Quora, Blogs, YouTube content, and books written on the subject.

Common Question: "How much does it take to get started on Amazon?"
Objection Handling Sales Copy: Find out how we can start Amazon businesses for WAY less than anyone else (and hear a crazy brand new hack that made the number lower than ever!), and why there is only ONE strategy to get started the RIGHT WAY on Amazon!

Common Question: "Can I sell on Amazon from another country?"

Objection Handling Sales Copy: Learn the secret to selling on Amazon from almost ANY COUNTRY IN THE WORLD. Learn the little-known way to sell on Amazon from anywhere, regardless of which country you live in!

The important thing about this is, I wouldn't have known what questions people had if I hadn't asked them. What you assume people's questions are and what people's ACTUAL questions are can be wildly different! Never assume! When you assume, you lose. When you assume, you know nothing. Trust the data, you win.

The Struggle Bus—All Aboard!

Sometimes, you can learn everything you need to learn about how to best serve your customers by asking just one simple question and looking for a pattern in the top three most common answers.

"What are you struggling with?"

Sometimes, people struggle with the wrong thing, and you, as the course creator, have to know when the causality is incorrectly rooted in a different issue.

Imagine you're teaching a course on how to start a successful blog. The majority of people you interviewed wanted to find out why they can't get enough traffic to their blog. Their struggle is real, but the main culprit might be that they don't know how to market correctly, or MORE LIKELY, they aren't writing content on the correct subjects that get more organic traffic or have a higher chance of going viral.

You, as the course creator, need to decipher the main questions and give them the best strategies to achieve their desired goal. This will make more sense with practice as you go along!

Becoming a master of understanding the initial pain and using it as a driving force behind initial questions/obstacles is the key to smoothly validating your course idea.

Focus everything you do on these three things, do them well, and you'll be successful:

1. Your Niche (Course Topic)
2. Offer (How You Can Help)
3. Desired Result (Where Your Customer Wants To Be)

Explain how you help people transition from their current situation to their desired situation. If someone's pain is their 9-5 job, and they want to make money online, you might say, "I can help you start your own Amazon business that will generate you a significant monthly income. Some of my students have been able to do this within as little as 90 days, if they're willing to put the work in!"

It's important to understand what you can do to help people get from point A (their current pain) to point B (their desired result).

Mastering Pain and Obstacles

Example 1: A course for corporate 9-5ers who hate their job and want to start a profitable online business.

The initial pain: "I hate my 9-5 job. I want a profitable online business."

So what are the obstacles?

Obstacle #1: "I need a profitable online business idea."

Obstacle #2: "How do I build my product or service idea?"

Obstacle #3: "How do people find out about my product?"

Obstacle #4: "Where do I sell my product or service?"

Obstacle #5: "How do I scale my online business?"

Finally, the pleasurable result is: "I have a profitable online business!"

Example 2: A course for recent moms on how to lose the baby weight and get back in shape.

The initial pain: "I am out of shape but want to look like I did before the baby."

So what are the obstacles?

Obstacle #1: "How soon can I start exercising after giving birth?"

Obstacle #2: "I'm too busy. How do I make time for exercise?"

Obstacle #3: "What exercises are safe for me?"

Obstacle #4: "I need an exercise routine I can do in 30 minutes or less."

Obstacle #5: "How can I make my exercise routine a habit and stay in shape?"

Finally, the pleasurable result is: "I'm in the best shape of my life!"

You need to understand the mental obstacles people use as excuses for why they can't do what you're teaching. You'll use this everywhere, in sales copy, in emails, in your webinar (if you make one), and when you're live in your group. You'll start to say it so often, you'll have it memorized.

You need to know the most common obstacles. It is your job to illustrate how to overcome them as simply as possible to reach the desired result!

Chapter 21

The Only Four Reasons
People Buy Courses

A s you start to have more success, your haters will ask, "Why would anyone ever buy a course from you when they can find all the information for free?"

Technically, you could go out into the forest, chop down trees, drag the trees back to your house, cut them into hundreds of smaller pieces, grind them up into a paste, dry them, treat them, and make them into paper. Or, you can skip all those steps and simply buy the paper in a grocery store, which is much more efficient and convenient. The same is true for a well structured, high-value course.

There are four main reasons why someone buys a course. It is important to understand these four and leverage them in your marketing materials!

Reason #1: Organization

Can you get the same thing for free? Not really.

When you sell an online course, you're selling information. However, you're not selling loose, unrelated pieces of information. You're selling a holistic system. You're giving people a proven method to learn a new skill or achieve a goal.

That's a lot more convenient for your customers than piecing it all together themselves. You'll find most people will happily pay for a proven system to take them step-by-step from point A, pain, to point B, pleasure.

Reason #2: One-on-One Help

When you sell an online course, you give each student an opportunity to ask you questions about the course. Not only are you selling information, but you're also offering people the chance to ask questions and get answers. You're offering both information and mentorship.

This interaction is what makes the difference. You could read a blog post and get some interesting advice, but if you have questions, what do you do? Email the blogger and hope they respond? They have no vested interest in responding, especially if you didn't pay them. If you bought a course from someone, guess what? They would respond. If you were selling an online course, I'm sure you'd respond to your customers, too.

Reason #3: Community

Many people who have taken my online courses agree that one of their favorite parts is the community aspect of the course. They like the feeling of being "in this together" with other people going through the course. They interact with each other, bounce ideas off each other, create masterminds and meet-ups with each other, and they hold each other accountable.

This is something you simply can't get if you just use free information you find on the internet. It's a perk people will happily pay for.

Reason #4: Accountability

Sure, if you devote enough time to it, you can teach yourself anything for free. People can go to the public library and find a book on any topic. But do they? No, they don't.

We live in a time when we have access to all the information we could ever want. However, consuming information is not the same as taking action. Most people just pick up a book or read a blog post, but they never take action on what they learn. So, what's different about an online course?

Well, paying for an online course is a commitment, and no one likes throwing money out the window. When people actually invest their money into an online training, they hold themselves more accountable.

For years, I never went to the gym. I knew I should have gone, but I just didn't do it. Now, I go at least twice a week. How did I build that habit? I hired a personal trainer. Paying him made me more likely to go—because I paid for it.

Chapter 22
Why You?
The Genuinity Complex

"The true method of knowledge is experiment."
— William Blake

How do you become the person someone wants to buy from?

In the onboarding fulfillment email I send to everyone who purchases my products, I ask every single person who has purchased my courses why they bought from me instead of one of my competitors, and where they heard about me. This is unbelievably valuable data!

About 1% say they bought because they wanted to learn about Amazon, Shopify, Facebook ads, or Digital Course Creation, and I had the best information. 99% say they bought because I seemed genuine, passionate, and they could relate to my story about feeling trapped at my 9-5 job. I gave them so much incredible information for free, they felt like they had to buy!

Facts Tell, Stories Sell

Before someone's going to buy from you, three things need to happen:

1. They need to feel like they know you.
2. They need to like you and feel like you're genuine.
3. They need to feel like they trust you and you genuinely want to help them.

Previous results can help them feel confident you have the things people need to feel comfortable buying from you.

Have you already gotten results related to your specific topic from yourself or others?

Whatever the topic is, you want to create a course around something you have gotten results for yourself or, even better, for yourself and for others. They don't need to be paying customers. It could be family members, friends, or coaching and consulting clients.

It is important that you can show results related to the topic you want to teach about in your course. Having proven results, even from friends, family members, or beta testers is so helpful!

Ideal Potential Students

Understanding your avatar is important. Different people feel like they know and can trust you in different ways. If you're selling a course about Medicare or insurance for seniors, then you want your online presence to be more professional than if you're selling a course on how to breakdance. Your ideal student avatar is drastically different in those two cases!

Similarly, if you're selling a course on how to shoot guns versus how to be an empowered woman, you would approach your customers differently.

How you present yourself and your course, your content, the words you use, examples you give, and your personality should be as close fitting to your perfect customer as possible. Don't overthink this. Be natural, but use your head!

At first, it might seem like having any and everyone inside your course would be awesome (and honestly, at first it is), but this is not the case at all. You'll find some students are more effort than they're worth. They'll think that for the $497 (or whatever you charge for your course) they paid, you should drop everything and become their personal butler.

To avoid this, it is very important to write a three or four sentence paragraph telling yourself (this is for internal purposes only) who the perfect fit for your course is. The same goes for initial consultations. As you do more and more, and get more and more students, you'll start to learn who is more effort than they are worth!

Removing Friction and All Reasons Not to Buy from You

Clean up both your personal Facebook and business Facebook pages. You want them looking professional, respectable, and up-to-date with no sketchy stuff, no random pictures of a dog as your profile pic, etc. Remember, you are a brand and a business now, and people make initial judgments based on what they see.

I used to hate wearing a suit for my accounting job, but now I wear one in some of my marketing because people make instant judgments based on clothes, images, and demeanor. You want to be aware of that and leverage it to your advantage.

Add a bio to your personal Facebook that easily summarizes your message to your audience, potential course buyers, and students.

I have included my intro as an example; however, mine is a bit different, since I already have so many students and multiple courses.

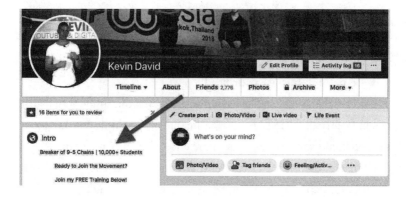

When you're first starting, you can define your message to the world with a simple sentence:

"I help (YOUR NICHE) to (DESIRED RESULT)."

For Amazon, it might say:

"I help Amazon Sellers Create Explosive Businesses on Autopilot!"

A piano can create sound, but if it's not playing the right notes, you're not hearing any music. It's very important to know that your message is resonating with your market. You want to make sure you and your audience are on the same wavelength, and your message is really striking a chord. Your properly tuned message is insanely powerful and will surprise you and your entire market.

In the next part of the book, you will learn about Facebook ads. You will need a Facebook business page to run your ads because all ads run from Facebook pages. Additionally, some people like to see if you are legitimate by checking to see if you have a well-assembled business page.

I normally use my company logo or professional-looking picture of myself as my profile picture, and a relevant, eye-catching image as my cover photo! Do not reinvent the wheel here. Find someone who has already been successful in your niche and play off what they have done, adding your own style!

If you're making a page for teaching eCommerce as your personal brand, search eCommerce. Use the Facebook search bar, filter by pages, look at the top ten most liked Facebook pages in your niche and see their cover photo, their profile picture, read their About section. Look at what they use for their Call to Action button, which we will discuss below. It might say, "Send a message to learn more and go to this website." Use it, with your own images and branding, of course!

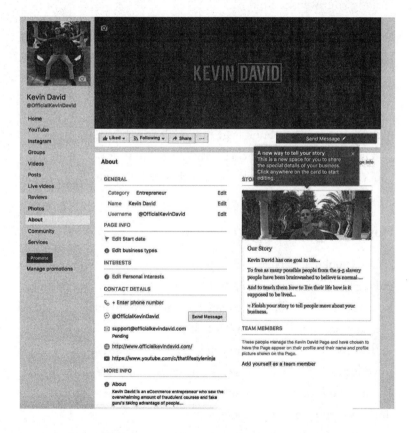

Create a minimum of 5-10 high-quality posts with eye-catching imagery or video that provide value to your niche. This doesn't have to be original content. Go to other successful pages in your niche, share their content on your own page and credit the original sources, or find popular blog articles on your niche. You just don't want your Facebook page to be completely blank; it looks sketchy. Start to put yourself in your future students' shoes. They want to make sure you're not a scam, so don't give them any reason to think you are!

Always include your website in the text of the post you write, so if it gets shared, people will see it and have a higher likelihood of clicking your website link.

How to Create Your "About Me" Section

Remember to edit the "About" Section in your group. This becomes your meta description in Google—or what appears as the preview text next to your Facebook page in Google search results.

Use relevant, highly searched terms related to your business and use your company URL. This also helps with Search Engine Optimization.

How to Add Your Call to Action

All Facebook pages have a CTA (call to action), including sending a message to a page or clicking to learn more and visiting a website. I have tested them all, and by far, the most profitable is the Send Message call to action. It works best if you have a customer service staff to answer questions (you can add a virtual assistant as an editor to your page or answer messages yourself). People are normally just one question away from making a purchase. Be there to ease their final concern before conversion.

At first, it will probably be you answering all of the messages, but as quickly as possible, you should hire and train a full-time virtual assistant to help with customer service and respond to messages.

Having 24/7 staff answering questions on my Facebook page is one of the single biggest conversion techniques I use for all my businesses!

A good way to get notifications on your phone when people message your page is to download the Facebook Pages App on your phone and turn on notifications. You will receive messages when people respond to your ads and/or message your page organically.

Remember, page messages are not normal messages and won't appear in your Messenger app; however, they do show up in the Facebook Pages App once you connect your page.

This whole time, you've been learning and doing research on your topic. You're learning everything you can about your audience and your customers, as well as their pains and desires. You're taking all your knowledge from what you already know: your experiences, blogs, books, YouTube, and Google. You've researched the people considered the mentors and gurus, who are leaders in this niche. Now it's time to get proof of concept!

Chapter 23
Establishing Proof of Concept

By now, you've absorbed all the most authoritative sources of information you can find. Your end goal will be making one fully organized master course, with an accompanying community that does one thing: gets your customers their desired result, even if they are a complete beginner, with no prior experience.

Let's quickly define the most important concepts to understand for this chapter.

Proof of Concept: Confirming that your efforts toward building a course are validated before starting by people showing enough interest in what you have to say to give you their "attention currency": to subscribe to you on YouTube, give you their email, join your Facebook groups, listen and respond to the content you create, and most importantly, pay you for your consultations or done-for-you services!

Minimum Viable Product (MVP): The most concise course you can make; less is often more, which has been proven by the software industry, and we are going to apply this ideology to our flagship course!

Proof of concept is three or more people paying for a done-for-you solution or consultation related to your niche.

Minimum Viable Product is the simplest course you can possibly create to take someone from their painful current situation to their desired result. Less is often more.

It is vital to understand that you can create a booming business only by establishing proof of concept and doing paid consultations and done-for-you solutions.

This is important to understand because it is a trap you need to be aware of. You will start to make more money than you perhaps ever have in the past, but it is critical that you keep the end goal in sight. Even though you will make nothing while you're building your course, and you can make a lot of money when you're doing consultations/done-for-you solutions, you have to remember the difference in scale!

Don't be drawn into the profitable allure of consulting and done-for-you solutions. That is not your goal—your goal is time and financial freedom. You want to actually be able to enjoy your newfound financial freedom with what is most important: the free time to enjoy it!

Consultations and done-for-you solutions involve dealing with people, require your manual efforts and time, and do not infinitely scale. Courses, on the other hand, *do* infinitely scale. So don't fall victim to the instant gratification as most people do, and never get around to making their course because they're making so much just doing their consultations.

The course is your only focus, proof of concept is just to establish interest in your course so you can feel confident you've chosen the right thing!

Before creating your course, you must get proof of concept.

A course is a massive amount of work to do right, and an even greater amount of work to change once you're done, and the biggest mistake you can possibly make is not testing your proof of concept before you set out to create your masterpiece.

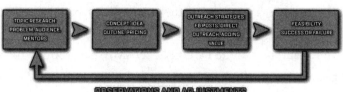

Think about it like this: If you spend 1,000 hours making a course on underwater basket-weaving and no one wants to buy it, you wasted your time.

Not only that, you've now sunk so much time and mental energy into courses that it would be nearly impossible to have the belief and confidence in the business model to ever do it again!

You MUST get a proof of concept and see if people you've added value for would be interested in an all-inclusive program, one that walks them from A-Z to get their desired result.

How do you find your first paying customers to establish proof of concept?

By using the strategies we discussed in Part 2:

Method #1: Facebook Posts

Post about your own personal success and your clients' successes daily. If you can't post about successes, post stories about business or your niche, questions, insights, tips, interesting articles and other details specific to your niche, what you are doing differently, and the current state of the market, or mistakes to avoid, generally helpful things!

You want to post in your Facebook group, on your Facebook Business page, and on your personal Facebook account for maximum visibility. I also like to post stories and go live on Facebook as they get maximum visibility. Be everywhere!

To get ideas, look at what the current most popular people or brands are doing and create your own content similar to that.

You want to say "(STUDENT NAME) went from flipping burgers at Burger King to making $10,000 per MONTH with (YOUR COURSE)!"

If you don't want your friends and family to see those posts, you can create what is called a friend list and add only potential clients or business people. Then, you can post statuses only they can see. However, I recommend posting to your whole friends list because you don't have to segment it, it saves your time, and it works better anyway.

It is important to get into the habit of saving all of your testimonials and success stories, even if they're just Facebook messages, Instagram messages, texts, Facebook posts, or video testimonials. The more you have, the better off you'll be! It's easy for them to get lost, so whenever you get one, screenshot it or download it. The first thing you should do is store it in a Google Drive folder.

Method #2: Direct Outreach

Direct outreach is sending an email, a Facebook message, a Linkedin message, any type of outreach to open a conversation with potential customers or people interested in your course!

If you're teaching accountants how to adapt to the digital age and make money, you can search online for them. Let's say you live in Dallas. You could search Dallas accountants on Google, find all of their email addresses in the footer of their websites, and email them, or find their social media profiles and message them there. You should become omnipresent, seen everywhere as often as possible, and make it hard for them to ignore you, even if they try.

Will some people say no or ignore you? Absolutely, but some people will say yes! They are who we care about. Nevertheless, getting told no a few times is a good experience.

Method #3: Adding Value + Answering Questions in Large Relevant Facebook Groups

This may be the single most effective way to get clients quickly. Join other people's groups, reach out to the owner, and ask if you can add free value to the group.

When you see questions from members, answer them! Provide thorough, thoughtful, well-researched, and well-written responses! Then create high-value posts teaching people how to do something you know they want to learn—this can be answering what you know to be the most common questions or concerns. It's a great way to feel out the market while adding value!

DO NOT include links or spam the group. You don't own this group. You want to add free value!

Contact them by saying, "If you have any questions, feel free to DM me!" People will message you if you are answering questions and adding value.

Holding Yourself Accountable

You need to be doing these things every day. To keep myself on track with this, I created a daily schedule. I know it's simple, but it helps to see what you need to do today to build momentum, find new customers and interested people, and start to incrementally accumulate that daily compound interest which will eventually pay off exponentially!

Sample Schedule:

Monday: Add 40 Targeted People on Facebook and Message Them + Make a Post on Your Facebook Group

Tuesday: Record and Launch a Proven YouTube Video Linking to Your Cheatsheet and Facebook Group

Wednesday: Add 40 Targeted People on Facebook and Message Them + Make a Post on Your Facebook Group

Thursday: Record and Launch a Proven YouTube Video Linking to Your Cheatsheet and Facebook Group

Friday: Do a Live Broadcast in Your Facebook Group + YouTube Answering People's Questions

These are just examples. I like to do one main thing per day, because switching between multiple activities is really hard for most people. Only you will know if you are consistent, and only you know if you're reaching out to 40 people per day.

You always get out what you put in. For every action, there is an equal reaction! If you reach out to forty people a day, you will be 2x as far ahead as people who only reach out to twenty, and the cycle continues!

When you do this, it builds massive momentum. You want to build invincible, unstoppable, immovable momentum that runs over and renders your competition completely irrelevant! You want to make your competitors an afterthought.

You want to post on your personal Facebook profile every few days. This builds momentum. Even if you get zero clients for your first few weeks, keep doing it. People will take notice, and they will reach out!

Invite your email list, even if it's one person, to a live training in your Facebook group once a month where you answer questions for everyone for free. All these actions will feel like massive resistance—

setting up a Facebook live for the first time, sending your first broadcast email—but it's going to get easier and easier. Before you know it, you're going to be a well-oiled abundance machine, set up the right way from the start!

Share student or client success everywhere, as often as you can! People get this wrong every day. They think they should post about their course and how great it is.

No one cares about you or your course. They only care about themselves and how you can help them. They only care about the results you're getting your students with your system because that means they could possibly get them too.

Once per week is generally enough to post student success stories, but if you have more than that, share them! Gather these testimonials in a centralized place like a Google Drive folder. The more you have, the better! You'll use them everywhere.

You want to start building up momentum like this. It might seem like you're not doing much at the beginning, and you might not get much interest on your first couple of days, but after you've built this up over a period of a few weeks, things are going to be happening for you. You're going to be getting results.

Every time I've tried to GUESS what the market wants, I've failed and lost money. Every time I think I know something, I find out that, actually, I don't know. Every time I talk to someone and understand what they want and need, I do know. It sounds pretty simple, and it really is.

With the invention and popularization of the internet, there is literally no excuse. At any time, your perfect customer is a message away on Facebook, or their email is on their website.

All the information you need to be successful is always just a few clicks away. It is just waiting for someone who hustles to find it and use it. That is either you, or it is someone else who climbs their way above you while you're watching Netflix. That is the simple truth.

Most of the strategies to establish proof of concept involve direct outreach to people in relevant Facebook groups, people who watch your YouTube videos, download your cheatsheets, or message you because of your high-value posts.

Step #1: Get people interested. Getting their attention is the HARDEST PART! Once you have their attention, you add value for free and built rapport.

Step #2: Convert their attention into a Proof of Concept. Sell them the fact that your consultation/done-for-you solution, and eventually course, will take them from their pain to their desires!

The Sales Paradox

To properly transition people from simply having their attention to investing their real hard-earned money, you need to understand the Sales Paradox.

Being able to communicate and sell an idea or a message is the most important thing in life and business, regardless whether it's selling yourself as a potential mate to a wonderful partner, or selling yourself on the idea to change your mindset and change your life. If you're thinking, "I'm not good at sales", or "I don't know how to make sales", or "Sales isn't for me. I'm definitely not a salesperson…" Answer me this: How many sales conversations have you had?

People have issues and feelings. They come in contact with you, via ads or organic means, and your ad, video, or Facebook post is designed to evoke emotion and help people.

You want to really hit them where it's most impactful—agitate their pain points. When you agitate their pain, they turn to you to provide a solution. You create a tangible separation between their current agitated, painful situation and the future state (or desired state). Then, you position yourself as the vehicle to that change. You're literally selling them the future. It's critical that you only use these methods ethically. These techniques are so powerful you'll be able to sell anything to anyone.

All sales, at the core, are thoroughly understanding someone's current situation, thoroughly understanding someone's desired situation, and then telling them whether you can help them or not.

People don't buy your services. People don't buy you. People don't buy your products. People are buying the future they want. People are buying a way out of their current situation and the pain they are in right now, and they're buying into their desired future and the state in which they want to be.

Even after eight figures of products sold (physical, digital, in person, on the phone, and online), my closing rate to this day is only around 30% for direct messaging or another phone type of transaction. If it's online only (ads to a funnel), its 1/10th of that!

After studying this, mastering hundreds of books about business and sales, and thousands of hours of my life, 70 out of 100 people I talk to in-person or over the phone say no.

After dedicating my life to sales mastery and digital marketing online, 97 out of 100 people who see my offers online say no. That is simply the way things work. You can be upset about it and lose, or understand it and win.

The good news is you have an *Unfair Advantage* in the form of a Sales Script, proven with millions of dollars of sales, available for free at: www.officialkevindavid.com/script.

Proof of Concept Paid Consultation Phone or Messaging Script

Sales is one of the most important things in any business because you can have the most awesome service or product in the world, but if you don't know how to sell, it's not going to be flying off the shelves.

Start off by clearly defining their current situation and their current state. Then, separate the current situation from the desired situation. Get clear data points for both of these things. That's what your role is on the sales call. Then, carefully position yourself and your offer as the vehicle to bridge the prospect from their current situation to their desired situation.

A profound lesson is that you're selling the future. You're selling people the future they want and desire for themselves. When you make the transition from selling products to selling futures, everything will shift for you.

Remember, when you're establishing proof of concept, there is a high chance you'll get ten no's in a row. Ten people in a row could tell me "no," and I couldn't care less. It happens; it's just numbers. If you get ten no's in a row, and then four yes's, you've proven your concept, and you're ready to start creating!

It's important to have at least a basic understanding of the math behind establishing a proof of concept. Three paid consulting clients is the minimum I suggest to establish proof of concept, but the more you have, the more solid your base.

You want to have the math understood in your head. If you want three or more people to establish proof of concept, assuming a 10% conversion rate, you need to directly and meaningfully send messages to thirty people to get those three to pay for your consultation or done-for-you service! That means you're on Facebook, in relevant groups messaging, actively contributing to those asking for help, or you're in direct outreach on Google, searching for "Plumbers in Dallas." You're contacting them all via email, phone, or Facebook.

Thirty is the bare minimum. Let's assume you decide to talk to one hundred people. Let's say you can talk to five people per day and want to talk to one hundred people. That would equate to twenty straight days of talking to five people to get ten paid clients at a 10% conversion rate. At that point, you've got a rock-solid proof of concept, and you can move forward with creating your course and everything that comes with it, knowing it has the highest possible likelihood of paying off!

Once you've got your *first* paid client, breathe a massive sigh of relief. That client is proof you're not just some crazy mad scientist, but what you're teaching actually works. Once you have your first three paid clients, you've validated proof of concept. These three people only bought because you've struck a common chord of interest.

Referrals are another, substantially underutilized strategy to establish proof of concept faster. The best way to get referrals is to set realistic expectations about what you're going to do for your clients, and then over-deliver. If you promise the moon, even if you deliver the moon, you're only going to meet their expectations. Happy clients are going to be indebted to you. Ask them if they have any friends, acquaintances, or coworkers who might need the service you provide as well. This essentially means you only need to find one paying client, and then you incentivize them to find your other two!

A proven way to increase a referral rate is to offer a referral bonus for each additional paying customer brought to you! For example, if you charge $500, you give a $250 payment per paid referral! Once you have your course going, you'll do this in a much more automated fashion with your affiliate program!

A lot of people come into this business thinking whatever they come up with on their first attempt should work. When it doesn't work, they believe they have failed. It's the wrong way to think. Nothing is a failure, it's feedback; failure only exists if you stop trying.

If we get a yes, awesome. We get a client, we make money, we get closer to proof of concept. If they say no, it's feedback, not failure. We need feedback to improve our process, our offering, and our message. We conduct our research and form a hypothesis. We test the market and collect feedback.

Your proof of concept offer should be limited in scope and should use as little of your time as possible for the highest value output!

To drive home the point, if you can get somebody results, everything else is noise. In the early stages, people are most willing to pay for a done-for-you solution. People are busy; they don't want to learn, they want it done, and they want it done right. They want it done fast with little to no input on their end.

Proof of concept for a done-for-you solution might be:

- setting up a Facebook ad campaign for someone's product or service
- allowing entrance into a private Facebook group about how to talk to women
- fully optimizing a Shopify store for mobile
- setting up a custom meal plan or exercise routine

Maybe you're going to create a course on how to make a website. Perhaps your offer would be to set up a basic WordPress site with an "About Us" page, a contact form, and social media links. If you want to sell a course on how to get washboard abs, you could offer an extensive cheatsheet with workouts or a meal plan PDF.

A paid proof of concept can be many different things, but the easiest and most effective are:

1. One-Hour Consulting Call
2. Done-For-You Solution
3. Access to Your Private FB Coaching Group
4. Digital eBook or PDF
5. Entrance to a Mastermind

The purpose of a proof of concept is to establish that you have found a winning idea through some exchange of money or a commitment to buy your course. If three or more people will pay for consultations or done-for-you solutions, they will also most likely pay for a self-service course and the community that comes with it.

These strategies are sure-proof ways to get quick wins. If you talk to one hundred people, even if ninety of them say no, ten of them will say yes—if you have chosen your target market correctly.

These quick wins are VITAL; human nature is inherently wired with self-doubt. We have to combat those natural self-doubts all humans have with quick wins to build confidence!

Everything changes when you get that first client. It's hard to describe until you experience it. Human nature forces you to question everything—it's an instinctual defense mechanism for self-preservation that helps keep us safe, which is why overcoming it is so difficult and important!

Most people, maybe even you, think, "Kevin can't possibly be right about all this digital course stuff, and proof of concept, and getting paid for consultations and done-for-you solutions. This might have worked for him, but it won't work for me. No one can really be making that much money selling a digital course. Why would people pay for my advice?"

These questions are natural and flow through everyone's mind until you get your first client! It's evidence that you've made the right decision. It's evidence that you are capable of doing this. It's evidence these methods I'm teaching you work.

If someone will pay you for your time on a consulting call, for a done-for-you solution, for mentorship, access to a private group, or for an eBook or PDF, that is the BEST proof of concept you can get regarding whether or not you have found a course that can work!

The key is to never allow yourself to get overwhelmed. Get some quick wins under your belt: sell a Blueprint eBook or PDF you made in a day for $19.

After two or three consultations, done-for-you service fulfillments, sales of your Cheatsheet, or access to a private Facebook coaching community, you start to feel some progress! Your three MINIMUM paid consultations would all ideally provide testimonials in the form of Facebook comments.

You want to have people comment about their experience working with you inside your Facebook group. If they can show before and after pictures or sales screenshots, that is ideal!

You also want to ask them for an under one-minute video testimonial. You will use these everywhere later on, so they are critically important. Nothing makes sales easier than social proof.

Setting Expectations

When you set expectations as to what people will receive, you will be happier when it comes to doing paid manual work, one-on-one consultations, or done-for-you solutions. The clients only want what was promised, nothing else.

When you don't set expectations, clients want everything and more, and even then, they'll not be satisfied. When you do set expectations, the clients will get exactly what you promised them. They'll end up staying longer, being happier, and paying more.

Good things happen when you set expectations, bad things will happen when you don't set expectations. You must clearly define costs, payment terms, hourly fees for additional work, and a minimum term if you have any, and the cancellation policy.

You don't guarantee anything, except the absolute best attempt to provide the service.

If you have no idea what to charge, then start out with $30-50 an hour (as this is a common entry point for USA based consultants).

If it's a single time fee, charge between $497 and $1,997 depending on the amount of work.

Another more minor, yet equally important, way to get proof of concept is to make a YouTube video or Facebook post on your course topic. See if people are interested enough to give you their email for your information. This may seem inconsequential, but it is actually a huge deal!

Ask questions to your potential customers. You can say things like, "Would you/have you previously paid $497 for a course that taught you how to make money selling on Amazon?"

You can also find the current largest influencers in your course niche and look at what groups they admin, and you can literally see how many people they have in their private group (meaning people who bought their course), and multiply that by what their course costs to get an idea of how much they've made. In my experience, about 60% of purchasers actually join the Private group!

Offer people who've commented on your videos, or are in your Facebook group, or have given you their email, a chance for a short, free call with you. If you don't have anyone in your ecosystem yet, go to Facebook groups or communities on your topics and start commenting on people's questions. Put thought into your answers and don't ask for anything—often times people will ask you if they can message you.

Chapter 24
You Da' Real MVP:
Your Minimum Viable Offer

"If I had more time, I would have written a shorter letter."
— Blaise Pascal

The most common temptation is to make a course on everything and to include every social media platform you can possibly advertise on, but this is a critical mistake.

What you actually want to do is to include as LITTLE information as possible to get your students from their pain to their desires in the most impactful way. Getting your students earth-shattering results, with the LEAST amount of information, is known as your Minimum Viable Product.

In the software world where people build applications and programs, there's a concept known as an MVP. As massive software companies were built, people added features, and they become more and more complex.

The software industry became a place where software companies would add as many features as possible because they thought this would make their companies more valuable, compared to their competitors.

The first version of the first course I ever created was called the

Amazon Ninja Course. I let three initial beta testers try it. At the time, the course was just a collection of scattered notes in Google Drive along with a Facebook group.

However, people loved the one-on-one attention I was giving them, and I quickly learned I needed something more scalable that could teach them without my direct attention 100% of the time.

Decision Fatigue

Everything good evolves from something that starts small and scrappy. Always err on the side of less, not more. Most failed software companies thought of their application as a picnic basket. They assumed the more they stuffed inside it, the better. They built a million different complicated features that were so overwhelming that no one touched them!

Something you have to constantly battle as a course creator is not allowing your students to get overwhelmed! Just because something is simple for you does NOT mean it is for someone else. Generally, the hardest part for most people is not the tactical portions, but the mindset required to actually get started to see some momentum build, to accumulate some quick wins, and to break THROUGH to the point of return for the incremental compound interest accumulation.

It is your responsibility to make numbered lists and break things into bite-sized chunks and sections in every way you can.

Think about Instagram: one of the most astronomically successful applications of all time, and all you do is post pictures. That is the core feature.

When McDonald's first started, it had only a few things on the menu. You could only get a hamburger, or cheeseburger and fries, and they only really had one drink. When it was like that, it was a machine, and it became the most popular fast-food franchise in the world. It took over the world. McDonald's has struggled recently in comparison to its explosive growth because it became bloated over time with a complex menu and too many options.

Think about it like this: which would be more difficult for you, going to the supermarket and choosing between two types of cereal or going to the supermarket and choosing between 100 types of cereal? One requires significantly more mental energy, and decision fatigue is a proven condition!

A few disruptive people came up with the idea called the Minimum Viable Product. That was the minimum amount of features required to satisfy the customer. For example, if someone needs an application to send emails, they build a Minimum Viable Product to send emails only.

Suddenly, these companies with MVP products started disrupting the companies with complicated software products. The users' responses were, "I'd rather have a simple software application than a big complicated one." The market started turning toward Minimum Viable Products instead of going with these big, fancy, complicated software programs.

Most people designing an offer think they need to throw as much stuff in this bag as possible, so people feel like they've really got a lot. That's INSANE!

So what are some examples of Minimum Viable Offers being worth more than more complex amalgamations?

Snapchat went from $0 to $16 billion in valuation in under 5 years, and what does Snapchat do? It doesn't perform complex calculations or solve world hunger, it allows you to send images and chats that disappear.

You can make the argument that it is declining in value, or had the perfect market conditions, both of which are probably true, but

99.99% of companies never reach a valuation anywhere near $16 billion, much less reach it in under five years. It focused on what it did best, and double and tripled down on that.

Often, companies that do less are worth more. It's just how it works. By doing everything, you're worth less. Complexity is overwhelming, and if you want to build something special, you have to play within the bounds of human nature. We want to utilize this knowledge when creating our course. You want to get someone from their pain to their desire in the most meaningful, life-changing way in the least possible time, and in the simplest possible way.

That is what your minimum viable offer is. An unbreakable, unstoppable focus on minimalism and high quality, to transport your customers from their pain to their desires in the least possible steps, with the least possible complexity.

Chapter 25
How to be "Beta" Than Your Competition

Most course creators will not beta test. It's a lot of work and takes time. However, if you really want to make sure you are doing this right and are a little uncertain about how to teach the content, what to include, what not to include, and you want focused feedback from people going through your course, then you are going to love a beta test. There is no better way to get direct feedback about your course regarding what is confusing, what needs additional clarity, and what is profound to people.

You can also get testimonial screenshots you can use everywhere in your marketing. When you have success stories, making additional sales is a piece of cake! Having a core group of successful students already inside your private group is amazing. Most people love the idea but don't actually do it. I personally do not beta test with every single one of my courses. I've gotten to the point where I am creating content for an audience I know really well. I am very certain when I come out with my new courses, they will do well.

Back in the day, I didn't feel that way, so I beta tested, and I'm glad I did. The ultimate validation of your expertise and ability to create a course is teaching one person to make money, find love, or get healthy! Obviously, you won't be working with everyone as intensely one-on-one, as your course starts to scale into the 10's, 100's and 1,000's of students, but you *can* start to help more and more people much more efficiently via live webinars and group calls.

In most experiences, the beta testers get to go through the program, cheatsheet, or blueprint for the course for free in exchange for their candid feedback, insights, and details about their results.

You don't want to come out with a program if you're not really certain it will get results. Beta testing will help you determine that really quickly.

Remember, you can make a significant amount of money simply from consulting with interested parties. Of course, the end goal is to make a fully automated, digital product because that is when true scale is achieved.

I want to make sure you understand that by getting the ultimate proof of concept, you can get the ultimate confidence to go full force into your course creation!

My advice to you is when you find your first interested parties, charge them $50 an hour, or $100 an hour to simply help them. If you can get real money in exchange for your knowledge, whether it is in the form of a course or in the form of consulting, you have taken an incredibly important step and destroyed a mental barrier, proving that this really does work!

I come across a lot of people who try to achieve their dreams as they are right now, without changing their ways, habits, and values. They really struggle because the person they are right now isn't the same person who will achieve those dreams. The path to achieving your dream, in REALITY, is dream, define, decide, design, daily actions, deliver.

📖 Part 3 Summary

- You learned about the top three questions your customers have and how to take your customers from their current state to their desired state.
- You learned about the mental obstacles your customers face and how to overcome them.
- You learned the four reasons people buy courses: organization of information, one-on-one help, community, and accountability.
- You learned the MOST common reason people who buy courses will buy courses from you: because you are genuine!
- You learned how to find your ideal customers, how to validate your course idea through proof of concept, and how to get three paid consultations or done-for-you services.
- You learned the concept of a Minimum Viable Product and that less is often more.

✅ Part 3 Checklist

- Have you found the top 3 questions beginners have about your course topic?
- What are the top 3 obstacles your customers think are stopping them from achieving their desired situation?
- Do you understand the 4 reasons people buy a course? Have you integrated that into your marketing materials?
- Do you understand the importance of being genuine and presenting yourself truthfully with regard to making course sales?

- Have you validated your course idea through proof of concept by getting at least 3 people to pay for a consultation or done-for-you service related to your course topic?
- Do you understand the concept of a Minimum Viable Product and how to apply that mentality to creating your consultations, done-for-you solutions, and ultimately, your flagship digital course?

If you're ready to get started with one-on-one help, now would be a great time to check out the Digital Course Secrets webinar to learn more! Go to www.digitalcoursesecrets.com/go now!

Part 4

Organizing, Pricing, and Building Your Course for Explosive Growth

Chapter 26

The Power of Organization and Change

"For every minute spent in organizing, an hour is earned."
— Benjamin Franklin

I f you do a poor or haphazard job of organizing your content without structure, meaning, or intent, people will notice, and they will be unhappy. Don't do yourself a disservice through laziness; spend proper time and put thought into organizing your course correctly.

Enjoyable Content

The communication infrastructure the internet provides has never existed before. This is either a really good thing or a really bad thing, depending on which type of company you have. If you have a dishonest, scammy company not providing any real value, and you don't care about your customers, you're not helping anyone. The internet will find out quickly, and you will drift into obscurity with unhappy customers.

If you're an honest company with an ultra-valuable product, the internet is a very good thing. Word of mouth will be your strongest ally and free source of never-ending marketing!

The truth is if people don't enjoy listening and learning from you, you've already lost, regardless of how good your content is. You need to remember people are busy, and there are now more options than ever. People have problems and issues, and if you can be their salvation from the chaotic, harsh world, you win!

If you can make learning enjoyable, you will have so many more success stories. When you have more success stories, you make infinitely more money!

Your content needs to do three things:

1. Keep your students engaged through your energy and passion.
2. Keep your students from being overwhelmed with structure and quick wins.
3. Create the best, most concise content you can after absorbing everything in the current ecosystem of your niche, combined and improved with your own knowledge and experience.

Your Skeleton

The order of the information you present is just as important as the information itself. When I create a course, I have a very chronological process I follow. I look at all previous top-tier, successful courses in my niche. I look at their table of contents and organization.

Look at Udemy courses, blog articles, and Google step-by-steps on your course topic. Look for similarities and patterns. If all of the successful courses share similarities in how they structure their information, that is a positive indicator of where you should start your skeleton as well.

Creating the skeleton just means a single sentence or bullet point showing how to organize information. I will bold these and then write notes underneath them as I am researching, learning, and adding my own experiences.

I try to add quotes and stories as often as possible because the human brain remembers information best with stories—and quotes become touchstones for people's learning, making them memorable and effective teaching methods.

There is always something out there to get initial ideas from, and if there is not—then maybe you chose the wrong course topic.

Be Open to Change

> *"If you aren't embarrassed by the first version*
> *of your product, you shipped too late."*
> — Reid Hoffman, founder of LinkedIn

You should never let yourself get writer's block from a blank canvas; other courses almost always have room for improvement. Use them as inspiration to get started and then build it your own way. Think logically about how someone with no knowledge of your current topic would think.

As you start adding information and creating your points for each module, you'll start to notice more efficient ways to structure the chapters. Sometimes I'll think, "Oh, this isn't really two chapters. This can just be put into one chapter."

Don't think it has to be exactly as you planned it in the beginning. Things are always open to change, and things are always open to being reshuffled and improved. Remember, the most successful people are the ones who are consistently becoming better versions of themselves. Similarly, your course will evolve and does not need to be perfect the first time around.

The most successful people are making constant incremental improvements to their daily habits, to their mindset and mentality, to their business, in their relationships, and in their lives.

You can't allow perfectionism to delay action. You must get started. It will never be perfect. One of the most common reasons I see people struggle and get stuck is just not getting started. Another reason people don't get started is that their past is haunting them— past failures and the pain associated with them.

This is a new day. You are a new you, and this is a new opportunity like nothing that has ever existed before. The knowledge economy is thriving like it never has, and you have a proven blueprint. If you consistently apply it as many others have, it will work—but you have to believe in yourself, trust the process, and do the work.

Your past isn't your present. The only way the human brain can understand anything is via comparison.

You wouldn't know what cold was unless you've felt warmth. You wouldn't know happiness if you didn't know sadness, because if you were only happy your entire life, it would be the only mindstate you had ever experienced; it would be your entire reality.

When I started to become successful, it helped me to picture my past as darkness, a tangible thing I could picture in my mind. This helped me understand the way I had existed in my past made it impossible to achieve my dreams.

Who I was then was not capable of achieving my dreams. With my previous mindset, my worldview, my daily habits, it wasn't possible. I really was a corporate drone. Society had beaten me into compliance, maintaining the status quo and being a worker. To achieve my dreams, I needed to transform my daily habits, who I was, my mentality, and my worldview to become someone entirely new.

It is difficult, but ultimately necessary, to accept and take ownership of the fact that who you are right now may not be capable of achieving your dreams. It was one of the most difficult things I had to accept, but it was the greatest realization of my life. You must evolve and become a better version of yourself to achieve your dreams. That means facing the darkness of your past and using that to define and intentionally move toward the light, which is achieving your wildest dreams. When you do that, you really do understand that you can do anything.

Rule of Opposites

People don't have business problems, they have personal problems that manifest in their businesses. If someone isn't committed to their business, you can bet they won't be committed to their morning routine, exercise routine, or daily habits.

If you have a messy car, you probably have a messy business. If you have an unhealthy body, you probably have an unhealthy business. I work from home, and in the beginning months, I noticed myself getting into the habit of not showering when I woke up, or shaving, or even getting dressed. I got lazy, and that laziness showed up in my business too.

Instead, I used the Rule of Opposites, and I chose to dress up in a suit one day. I felt and looked sharper; I shaved and put on deodorant. I felt amazing, and my business reflected that!

Changing your daily habits is how you change your future and become your better self. Quite often, the best way to change your habits is with the rule of opposites. It breaks you out of autopilot where you go about your day without realizing how programmed you are.

I want you to do something right now. Take out your phone and choose the app you use most often. I want you to move it to a different place on your screen. If it's on the first page of your phone, put it on the second; if it's in the top left of your phone screen, put it on the bottom right. Start to take note of how much mental energy it is to open it compared to before.

The reason it takes more mental energy to find and open it after you move it is that you have formed neural pathways and have habituated where it was on your phone screen. The same thing holds true if you have a gym or go to work. How often do you take different paths to work?

Most people take the exact same path every single morning because it's easier from a brain functionality perspective. It requires less brain power to take the same path. The rule of opposites breaks you out of that autopilot mode and allows you to make significant changes in your life.

If you've always had a messy office, clean it up. If you've always been an extrovert, do something quiet and reflective. Go drive to the beach or the forest. Go somewhere by yourself, because often extroverts never get any time to quietly reflect and think about what the essence of their work is.

A lot of people who are introverted and really understand their work need to be more extroverted, so they can go out and communicate with other people about what they're selling.

By buying into the rule of opposites and breaking out of the daily autopilot (we all have it), you can learn more about yourself in a few days than you can in years of letting your subconscious mind dictate your daily actions.

Even when you achieve tremendous success, you still need to discipline yourself. You need to make sure you show up to work. You must treat it seriously. When you take your life seriously, it will reflect in your business, and you'll see tremendous success!

Chapter 27
From Skeleton to Flesh and Bones

"Art is the elimination of the unnecessary."
— Pablo Picasso

To start creating your course, it is best not to reinvent the wheel. There are other courses, and people have spent hundreds of thousands of hours thinking about the best way to organize the same information to be palatable to beginners!

It is your responsibility to research exhaustively the most popular content on your niche topic, cross reference other courses to find patterns of information organization, and then make improvements based on your own knowledge or experience!

The Grandma Test

If you can't find anything at all using the previous strategies of looking for pre-existing outlines and chronological tables of contents, then you need to have a moment of reflection about your course topic and whether it's the right choice.

If your course topic has absolutely no other content to review, to get an idea of organizational structure, use what I like to call the "Grandma Test."

You want a proven course topic. If it's possible to make money, it's likely someone has done it in one way or another. However, if you're sure of your topic and can't find anything, use the Grandma Test. Start brainstorming your outline and presenting it in a way that even your sweet, old grandmother who knows nothing about the subject could understand.

Take Amazon, for example: most people (I learned through my free 15-minute consultations) think Amazon.com sells every product on Amazon. So, a common belief we need to shatter is that only Amazon sells products on Amazon.

I might start by saying, "Did you know most products sold on Amazon.com are sold by everyday people like you and me?"

Have a moment of reflection, "Okay, so now that I know anyone can sell on Amazon, where would I start if I wanted to start selling on Amazon? What is the first thing I would need to do? Find a product that could make me money!"

The next questions would be:

- How do I start looking for good products to sell?
- Is there any software I need?
- Once I find a product, where the heck do I order it for cheap?
- How do I ship it from China to the US?
- Once it's in the US, how do I make my product listing?

Managing human nature is one of the most difficult parts of building a successful course, even more so than creating the content or technology itself. Keep that in mind when you're creating your course and everything contained inside it!

Writing a course outline serves as a method to force me to organize my thoughts into a step-by-step methodology. When it comes time to film the course, I can follow along with my course outline, which makes filming the easiest part.

People love having both videos and PDFs or written notes. It feels like a larger value, and it gives people the additional structure all humans crave. You can easily tell the difference between a course that has been mapped out and one that is off the cuff. It's night and day. You want to do it right, even though it is more upfront work. Your course will have a far longer life if done correctly!

The skeleton is your chapter titles and parts. It might look like this:

Chapter 1—Understanding Facebook Ads & What Works + Vocabulary You Need to Know + The POWER of the Ninja Pixel Strategy!

Part 1: How to Create a Facebook Page (NEEDED TO RUN YOUR ADS!)

Part 2: How to Optimize Your Facebook Page Settings and Add Your CTA!

Part 3: How to Set Up Business Manager (The Advanced Way to Run Facebook Ad Campaign)

Organizing with numbered lists and by chapter helps break your course into bite-sized pieces that people can implement without getting overwhelmed.

Creating a detailed outline takes significantly longer than simply recording videos, but it ensures a more beautifully structured course. If you don't organize your thoughts into written form, the outline becomes scattered.

If your course is beautifully organized, you will benefit immeasurably through word of mouth for its greatness! Putting the work in up front will make you more in the end through a quality product and user experience, which will give you additional word of mouth marketing!

You can also give your beta testers just your written course outline and see what their questions are and their suggestions for improvement. Each time I make a course now, I ask successful students who are ready to fully commit to my new course to come on board as a beta tester for free!

Chapters and Parts

I like to create five chapters, with a minimum of ten parts per chapter. It can be tempting to make hour-long videos with everything, but trust me, your refund rate will go down if you split your thoughts strategically into multiple videos. It feels like your students are getting more for their money, even if it's the exact same content split into multiple videos!

My courses start with an introduction explaining the course, the private student group, and how important it is to be involved there. If you get your students to buy into the private community you create, your course will become infinitely more valuable. It is critical your students join and participate in your private group.

In your welcome video, you also want to discuss how to absorb the course content, whether your students should watch the full course before implementing, or if they should implement as they go.

I always like to include student success stories at the beginning of the course to show my new incoming students that it is not only possible but happening often! You want to have each part of your course answer the main questions and objections for the majority of your audience.

Summaries are incredibly important. At the end of each chapter, I like to create a checklist with action items they need to have finished after completing the chapter and a summary of the most important points from the chapter.

This gives a sense of closure for the material learned, and shows people what must be implemented to actually achieve success with the program. If you ignore these, people just get lost in a maze!

You want to include only the three or four things that matter most because that allows people to adjust. There's a lot of chaos going on in most people's lives. They might have a family, they might have other business things going on, people are blasting them with emails and marketing to them, and so on.

Your purpose is to use your Minimum Viable Offer to get them from Point A (their current pain) to point B (their desire) in the least possible time, with the least possible effort!

Idea Branding

The power of idea branding is truly remarkable. When you go beyond just passing on information, you can create content that's memorable and unique— that's what makes a good course great. This isn't hard to do. You can take any piece of advice, tip, or technique, put your stamp on it, and make it stand out. It's worth it because idea branding can turn run-of-the-mill content into exceptional, memorable content. It also ensures that people will credit you with the idea, strategy, or technique you brand. You can use metaphors and/or make your own unique names/acronyms for things such as KISS (Keep It Simple, Stupid!).

When I first started teaching Amazon, I called a method I used to track inventory the iTrack 999 Cart Trick method (This was before I even knew about idea branding. I just needed something to call it!), and I see it being used in the Amazon community by people I've never met to this day! That is the power of idea branding!

You can call things anything, but my method is to refer to whatever I'm teaching as the "XYZ," followed by one of these words:

Approach Blueprint Concept
Formula Framework Method
Model Plan Principle
Process Routine Strategy
System Technique

For example: the Amazon Blueprint or the Inventory Forecast Framework. This way, your students can refer to common ideas and portions of your course quickly and remember things effectively. They will also refer to these things by name in questions in your private group, which makes it easier for you and others to address!

Remind your students why they signed up for your course in the first place to give them the added motivation to start and finish your course. Refer back to the research you've done about your audience and the feedback you received from your "Irresistible Free Thing" to describe what's really driving your students to want to solve the pain your course solves.

Chapter 28

How to Create Success Stories

"Writing is thinking. To write well is to think clearly.
That's why it's so hard."
— David McCullough

You have to not only teach people, but you have to keep them engaged, accountable, and motivated.

The Importance of the Welcome Video

The goal of a welcome video is to get your new students excited, set yourself up as the leader, and remind them that they are exactly where they need to be. In the video, tell your students how you will teach them inside the program. Let them know how you want them to go through your program. Can they skip around? How much time should they devote each week?

Remind them of the time commitment. Your goal is to get them through the program.

Address the fears or concerns that might creep up while your students go through your program. Give them a plan of attack. Above all else, inspire your students! Remember, your mindset is just as important as your content. Spending time here will save you tens or potentially hundreds of thousands in refunds. It puts the responsibility on the student.

The Importance of the Private Facebook Group

You want to think of your private group like your family. If you really believe in it, and others do too, you'll have a very happy life. If your students are just money in your pocket, they will feel like that. If they are your family, they will act like that and become your best marketers. You want to incentivize people to join the private group. This can be with an additional free bonus or even to claim their course access.

I've seen course creators only give the membership link inside their Facebook group to force joining because sometimes 30-50% of people don't join the private group, which is crazy, but that is just the way things are!

You have to give them an incentive to do so, such as one-on-one help, a free bonus, or access to the course. It is critical that you do this because without your private group, your success stories will be infinitely lower. It's harder to help your students one-on-one, and they don't see the social proof of your other success stories (and get motivation) from them.

You also want to incentivise your students to talk about their success. I had a student in my Facebook ads masterclass recently who went from $4k a month to $400k+ per month using the strategies I taught. He never told me and never joined the private group. I found out through one of my inner circle members and had to track him down!

Who Doesn't Love a Good Bonus?

You can't have success stories if you don't have people join your course. The best way to get people to take action and join your course is with bonuses. People will find any excuse to do anything in the world rather than make meaningful decisions and commitments (which means buying your course).

People are terrible at making decisions and procrastinate by instinct. It's human nature, but we have to combat that. One of the strongest tools in our arsenal, other than scarcity (which we will discuss in the marketing chapter), is the use of bonuses—people can't stand missing out on bonuses. I can't even describe to you how many emails I've gotten from frantic people making sure they won't miss the bonuses if they buy right now!

Bonuses are incredibly important. People have been trained for years to love sales and value, and to love "free" bonuses.

These will be used in your webinar, advertised on your sales and order pages, and used in your Facebook posts when you open your beta. They should become a part of your everyday marketing arsenal. You want to make your free bonuses as valuable as you possibly can!

For example: in my Facebook course, I included bonuses on Facebook Messenger bots and Instagram advertising. These hugely popular topics have a lot of buzz as being the next best thing, which most people can't resist!

Chapter 29

No Excuses: How to 10x Your Productivity and Output

Little Task Devil

The little task devil (LTD) is an incredibly important concept to understand. The little task devil will try as hard as he can to distract you. He comes in many forms, such as housework, your 9-5 job, your current clients, other books, Netflix, and things you know are distracting you but still end up taking up all of your time.

Because you know that building a following and course is the most profitable possible use of your time, you have to become aware of the little task devil and make sure he doesn't control your life. When little tasks like emails, phone calls, and errands come your way, dedicate one day to them all (if you can't avoid them), and knock them out!

You cannot allow them to interrupt your deep work time. The little task devil will try as hard as he can to distract you from the highest possible ROI for your time, so be aware of him, and keep him under control!

The way I do this is by starting my workday with my most important task. If you don't know what it is, it's probably what you're procrastinating doing (YouTube or building your Facebook group by adding forty targeted people per day).

You have probably never done YouTube before, or have never reached out to new potential customers on Facebook to build your Facebook group. You're nervous! Because you've never done it before, it requires new neural pathways to start, which is why it's hard!

You procrastinate doing it because it's hard, but when you're self-aware about these things, you can nip the bad habits in the bud and defeat the little task devil! Get in the habit of starting your workday with your most important task; do not let yourself get lost in the details!

Block out entire days to work on specific tasks. Don't multitask.

The way to achieve results is to not focus on it. It's to focus on the process that generates the result. Go dark to get things done.

If you have a deadline or a big project to deliver on, remove yourself from the world.

Stay inside, turn off your phone, and don't touch email or social media. Don't come back to reality until the project is done.

Take Responsibility

Remember, where you are in life right now financially, physically, and mentally is precisely how you have designed it.

YOU are responsible for where you are in life right now. What you have right now, how much money in your bank account, the state of everything you have is because of you.

I'm not here to console you and tell you everything will be perfect and alright. I'm going to give you the mindset and tactical tools to be a winner and to revolutionize not only your business but your life.

I think about it like a video game. You're choosing to play the next level of life. This next level is harder; it is not comfortable and easy. You can't expect level 2 to be as easy as level 1, or it wouldn't be any fun. We are going to go to level 2, and 3, and 4. But to do that, you WILL face resistance, you WILL leave your comfort zone, and you'll come out on the other side stronger, happier, and more fulfilled. Don't drown in tools and software and the next shiny object. Don't "Guru Hop." If you look at what people are DOING and not what they are saying, you will realize those making the most money are doing so selling their courses.

When you understand the motivation behind WHY people say things, you get to the truth much faster! Use what works, nothing more, nothing less.

Chapter 30

A Picture Paints a Thousand Words, But a Video Makes Millionaires

I love painting as a hobby, but sometimes it's fun to become a millionaire and impact thousands of lives, wouldn't you agree? A video makes people fall in love with you. They feel like they know you and are friends with you in a way that can't be replicated on any other medium. I can't describe to you how many times I've met my students or other people who've recognized me from YouTube and they all say the same thing: "I feel like I know you!"

For people to buy from you, they have to feel like they know and trust you. The fastest way to build rapport and accomplish this is through video, which is why YouTube is the most powerful platform in the world.

Your membership platform is where you prove that the money your students spent on your program is worth it!

99% of the videos I create are screen share, where the viewers are seeing my computer screen as I share information. Another massive benefit of spending the time to organize your thoughts and course structure on paper is that when you go to record your videos, you can just follow your own outline and add additional clarity, more examples, and flesh out what you introduce in deeper form.

Most of the videos I record are done in a single take, but the only possible way to do this efficiently is to have my outline fully completed. Videos are perfect for tutorials for technology, ie. more intense technological walkthroughs that are difficult or time-consuming to create in text format. Just leave yourself notes in your course outline that says it will be discussed in detail in the videos!

Consider the power of certainty—when two people propose the same two ideas, the person who seems more certain will win 100% of the time.

I say this because you are now the expert. You are no longer able to say "it depends." People want to be told exactly what to do, which means you need to evaluate choices and give your well-researched and educated opinion on software, the best way to do something, etc.

Once all chapters and lessons within chapters are created with accompanying documents, you need to start recording one video screenshared for each lesson, and edit and export each video. Name the exported video the same thing as the lesson title it corresponds to (this will save you so much time).

Wrong Is Sometimes Right

Whenever you put something out there for the first time, it feels all wrong. When I first created the Amazon Ninja course, it felt wrong. I didn't know if I included enough content or not enough. When I first did a YouTube video, it felt wrong. When I first got on the phone and did a consultation for proof of concept, it felt so awkward and wrong.

That's just how it always feels in the beginning. It's important that you take imperfect action because taking big leaps forward feels like that. A funny thing happens the second time you make a course video, a YouTube video, or do a consultation call; it starts to feel just a little bit easier, and the next one is even easier. That is how you learn and grow as an entrepreneur and a person.

It has become commonplace to mold the situation to fit you. However, often times it's YOU who needs to change. I've witnessed over 10,000 people come through my trainings and have grown myself from absolutely nothing, with zero followers on any social media, to hundreds of thousands of followers and more than $10,000,000 in less than two years.

I have no fraction of a doubt that I could make hundreds of millions of dollars if I desired. I've made a massive transformation for thousands of people; it's not a random act of luck. It's because I chose to make a mental evolution. When your mindset evolves, your life quickly follows.

Take responsibility for your life, your actions, and your thoughts. Understand that where you are in life right now is all your doing. You've built the person you are right now. It was you.

Society often tells you to just "be you," to accept what you have been given, and to not "forget where you came from." Interestingly enough, the second I started to achieve success, my friends from the past said, "Kevin, you've changed!"

It is human nature to question yourself when you see people achieve success around you, because you start to think, "What am I doing wrong? How did he leave the cubicle while I'm still here?"

When people question themselves they start to panic. Most people don't like change. They like to stay where they are, inside their comfort zone, and they often attack you when you try to leave because they fear your success. Your success makes them question themselves.

Society tells you to stick to your roots, be yourself, just be you, be authentic. I'm sure you've heard it a thousand times.

I've come to realize that if you just teach someone to do Facebook ads, they might go from $5,000 a month to $10,000, but they don't have earth-shattering, life-changing results.

The people who refuse to change anything about themselves, about their MINDSET and worldview, who just want to make a few more dollars a month never get life-altering results.

The people who are open-minded about making improvements and focus on their mindset, rather than the money, are the ones who end up making the most!

Some of the most successful people on Earth will admit they made who they are today. Tony Robbins often says he wasn't born Tony Robbins; it's not who he is, or his roots. He's not just being himself, he MADE Tony Robbins incrementally over time through self-reflection, careful analysis, and consistent effort. Becoming truly great requires consistent incremental effort.

Michael Jordan wasn't just born with a basketball in his hand as the best player on Earth. He had to evolve and grow into that. In fact, he was cut from the varsity team in high school. Think about what that would have done to most people. They probably would have given up.

Most people told him he'd never be good, but he still did it. We're all born the same way, as helpless babies. We have to go out and get the skills and knowledge we require, no matter what anyone says or thinks!

Chapter 31
Becoming a Maestro of Pricing

"Perhaps the reason price is all your customers care about is because you haven't given them anything else to care about."
— Seth Godin

Something all course creators (including myself) go through is the guilt of charging for what you know. It is natural to feel guilty and uncomfortable at first about selling what you know, literally charging for information in your brain. Understand that human nature makes us feel this way. Reflect and observe it rather than feeling it personally. Hundreds of millions of dollars exchange hands for information products. If you don't capture that value, someone else will!

When I first started, I was terrified to charge other people for my knowledge or my consulting. I noticed that what I was confident charging other people was an exact match to the amount I was confident investing in myself. I invested $1,000 into an online course, so I felt confident charging $1,000. If I joined a mastermind for $5k, I was confident charging $5k for a mastermind. I really started to recognize a pattern. The prices you're confident charging others are really just a mirror reflection of the prices you're comfortable investing in yourself.

Think about college. It is perfectly acceptable to charge someone $50,000 a year to learn often outdated information from professors who can be apathetic and are nowhere near as passionate as you will be teaching your students.

When comparing a $50,000 per year college, where you learn antiquated information from overpriced textbooks, all of a sudden charging $997 or $1,997 sounds like an amazing alternative if it can jumpstart a career (often times more lucrative than college would!).

You may be surprised that people right now are charging $99, $1,000 or even $50,000 for knowledge products. How could anybody do that?

Well, think about it. Have you gone to college? How much does it typically cost for one class? Often, one class costs thousands of dollars.

A class at a community college might be cheaper, but it is still hundreds of dollars. Imagine the impact your content could have on someone's life. What is it worth?

When you start to create a more successful business, sometimes little ideas or one new tool or strategy can increase your earnings by thousands, so the value of the course changes. If your course earns someone $100,000, is it worth $100,000?

An incredibly important mind-shift is understanding that what you're teaching is worth more than the money it costs. Because when you understand and BELIEVE it, you no longer feel the "seller's guilt" everyone naturally feels when they charge for their knowledge.

I know it might seem awkward to charge for your course, but first of all, it is how you're going to get paid, and secondly and much more importantly, it is how you are going to hold people accountable to their goals.

I was in New Zealand recently, and there was only one gym in the small town where I stayed. It was over 250 USD per month because it was the one gym, and it knew that people would pay it if they were desperate. I grudgingly agreed to pay it, and you better believe I was in there every single day to get my money's worth!

The same holds true with your course...

When you pay, you pay attention. If you gave it away for free, no one would ever use it, but when they pay for it, they want to ensure they get their money's worth by working hard; it's human nature! This is SO TRUE!

Your course is extremely valuable if built correctly with vast amounts of knowledge, and charging for it is more than fair. To set a baseline, take a look at what others in your niche are charging. You might learn some people are charging $67 per month, while others are charging $497, $997, or $1,997. Try to find 5-10 others selling courses and formulate an average.

HOW TO PRICE YOUR ONLINE COURSE

	A "TELL PEOPLE WHAT TO DO" DIGITAL COURSE	A "SHOW PEOPLE HOW TO DO" DIGITAL COURSE	A "SHOW PEOPLE HOW" DIGITAL COURSE WITH 24/7 COMMITTED SUPPORT
A SMALL PROBLEM SOLVING COURSE	$0-$47	$48-$97	$98-$297
A MEDIUM PROBLEM SOLVING COURSE	$97-$297	$297-$497	$498-$997
A LARGE PROBLEM SOLVING COURSE	$297-$497	$498-$997	$998-$4,997

Establishing Your Pricing

Confidence: You feel confident about your price point. It has to be something that you feel excited about and in your heart (and in your gut) you know you are getting paid what you are worth.

Loyal Customers: You must be willing to deliver 10X the actual value you are promising. This is how you create wildly loyal customers who tell all their friends about you.

The Perfect Clientele: The price point you choose must demand the kind of clientele you want to attract. The minimum you should charge for your course is $47, for something that takes less than a month to create and is mainly for the purpose of getting new people into your ecosystem!

Let's say you realize your average is $397, but there are people selling for $197 and some selling for $997.

I have very strong feelings about this next part, so let's have another quick story…

Once I bought a necklace for my girlfriend. I wanted it to be the best. I narrowed it down to two necklaces that looked similar.

One was $19.97 while the other was $99.95. Even though the necklaces looked almost indistinguishable, I ended up buying the more expensive one because people associate price with value. It's why jewelry businesses exist and flourish!

I always want to be the most valuable course out there. I go above and beyond what others offer from a value perspective, from a one-on-one perspective, from a resources perspective, and from an update perspective.

I want to be the luxury option because it generally takes the same amount of effort to attract 1,000 people to your course, and if you sell 3% of them at $997, or 10% of them at $47, it's a wildly different amount of money over the long term!

My Favorite Pricing

I've tested everything, subscription plans, selling portions of a course, all the way from $97 to $20,000 and there is no question in my mind, the $497 to $1,997 range with NO DISCOUNTS are by far the best.

If you ever do a discount for Black Friday or Christmas, people WILL get upset with you if they recently bought for full price. It can have a permanent effect on the perceived value of your course, which is why I prefer to never discount!

If you have a course on how to make money, you can demand these prices. If you have a course on fitness, or something nonfinancial, your pricing might be significantly lower and your business model will thrive off volume rather than being high-ticket, but the same ideas hold true.

If your competitors were all charging $19 or $47 a month, you would want to do $97 a month for way more value and one-on-one help.

I know selling may not be your favorite activity, but when people pay you, it gives them the transformation they need to change their lives.

Let's do some math to illustrate just how big this can get if you get your traffic down—how many website visitors do I need to make five million dollars at a 1% conversion rate?

If your product costs $5 you need 100,000,000 visitors (not realistic).

If your product costs $1,997 you need 250,000 visitors (more realistic).

Generally, the sweet spot for courses is $497 to $1,997, anything under that and you're not maximizing your traffic conversion percentage, and anything over that, and you need a sales team and phone closers.

People are accustomed to the $997 price point. If you're making a course that solves a big problem or makes people money, this is where you should price it!

This doesn't apply to every niche, obviously. There are courses on nutrition and self-education that will be much cheaper, but it's important to understand that distance equals money.

The further you take someone in their transformation, the more you can charge for your courses. I've tested the absolute hell out of this, and $497 or $997 is the sweet spot. There isn't a significant difference in conversion, so I would just do $997 unless you feel strongly about $497, or your niche is outside the Make Money Online niche. If you want to price lower, I would recommend $197 at a minimum and the sweet spot at $497.

Look at what the most popular people in your niche are doing price-wise, compare the top three, and then make it better.

Never price the lowest; be the premium brand.

Mindset Matters

Promise me three things:

1. Become a Passionate Learner: Sometimes the BEST way to learn something fully is to teach it.
2. Confront and overturn your limiting beliefs and create a new worldview that allows you to venture out of your comfort zone.
3. Stick to the process and take consistent daily action until compound interest exponentiates your results. Compound interest is one of the greatest forces on Earth, and you now have the unique knowledge to leverage it into vast amounts of money and, more importantly, impact on your future students! You can't afford to lose this for a day because when you lose sight of your dream, you will become a part of somebody else's dream really quickly!

Mindset Shift: Someone asked me, "Kevin, what is the most vital life-changing piece of advice you could possibly tell us that made you successful?"

I knew the answer immediately—it was that I didn't give up.

I chose all of the wrong things.

I tried to make an iOS app, which was wrong...

I tried to start an online travel blog called EatSleepTrekRepeat, which was wrong...

I tried monetizing niche websites with Google Adsense, which was wrong...

I did everything wrong, but by doing all the wrong things, I eventually found the right things, and then I was able to remember what the right things were. I just journeyed through every possible variation, found out what worked and what didn't, and eventually got to this point. What would have happened if I had done everything wrong and given up *before* I broke through and found what worked?

I also realized I had evolved into my next form. I am no longer the same person I was while listening to orders in my cubicle. I have become someone who questions the status quo and doesn't listen to the hivemind. Rather, I have learned to think for myself and come to my own conclusions through careful experimentation and self-reflection.

I remember meeting one of my original students. She was in her 40's, shy, at a corporate job, and had been literally brainwashed by society and the cubicle life for decades. I thought to myself, "She is going to have a hard time making this work..."

But the thing I didn't realize was that she is not the same person now as she was. She is a totally new person. She used to think success was climbing the corporate ladder, and now she's making 30k a month from home, which is significantly more than she was at her corporate job working significantly fewer hours, even after decades in the workforce.

The funny thing is, I did the exact same thing. I am completely different than I was when I was trapped inside the cubicle at PwC.

One person lacked confidence, didn't think outside the box, didn't question the status quo and the way things were done. He was self-centered and expected the world to change for him without changing himself. He thought money was difficult to get, and that he should save money because that is how you get more money.

Now, all that has changed. I live each day to the fullest, I enjoy my life and everything inside it, people speak about me differently when I'm not around, women and men respect me more, and I interact with the world with newfound and well-deserved confidence.

Chapter 32

The Internal Battle: Your Lazy Mind Vs. Your Conscious Mind

The internal battle of your Lazy mind vs. your Conscious mind is the most important thing to understand when you're trying to evolve as a person. When you learn to control your lazy mind, you instantly become 100x more powerful.

Imagine how your friends would talk about you in a casual setting without you. What would they say about you? That you could be successful but don't apply yourself? That you drink too often? That you just lack focus?

Even if your friends don't know your bad habits, YOU do. This is how you would define your current character, what you stand for, and how the outside world perceives you.

Let me illustrate with an example. Let's say it is first thing in the morning, right when you wake up, and the first thought that pops into your head is, "You can go back to sleep, you can cancel your meetings and do them tomorrow," or "You've already got enough money for this month, you could just not do anything and watch movies all day..." Those are the FIRST things that come into your mind, but that isn't you, that isn't your conscious mind, that is your lazy mind. Everyone has it, but not everyone has learned to control it!

You have to learn to recognize it and say to yourself, "No, I'm not going to let my lazy mind get away with that!" Sometimes, I will audibly say, "NOT TODAY, LAZY MIND!" Then, using my conscious mind, I physically force myself to get up out of bed and go to the gym, or to the shower, or start my workday.

I know that sounds ridiculous, but you have to gamify your habits. When it's a game and you're in a competition with yourself, you're much more likely to be consistent and WIN!

I think about it as a competition. I'm not going to let my lazy mind win. I'm going to beat him, and I'm going to do it every day. If you do it enough days in a row, your life starts to seriously change for the better.

Think back to high school. How much easier did it seem waking up early every morning than in college when you didn't have to? It's because you formed habits and your circadian rhythm synced with those habits, providing you energy.

This is extremely powerful to understand, because you no longer fall victim to the lazy and doubtful voices in your head telling you to give up, or not talk to that beautiful girl at the bar, or not push as hard as you can push; things start to change!

The Self-Doubt Devil

Self-doubt is the ultimate killer of success, evolution, and growth as a person. You have to understand that self-doubt is nothing but a devil in our ear that wants us to fail and be average forever.

When you take a step back and see the "self-doubt devil" trying to sabotage you and drag you down, and you RECOGNIZE self-doubt is just an illusion, that is when you can grow. You can say, "Not this time! I recognize you, self-doubt. I'm going to trust the data and put the work in every day until my beliefs become my reality!"

All of us have self-doubt, but the more experiential success and small wins under your belt, the easier and easier it becomes to IGNORE self-doubt and recognize it for what it is!

Self-doubt evolved in the human brain to protect us from real-world physical danger such as predators; we evolved instincts to protect us, to DOUBT our decisions, thus increasing the likelihood of making the right one, staying safe, and continuing our species.

Now that we live in a modern society where there isn't impending physical danger and predators around every corner, we don't need it anymore, so we have to kill it, and kill it fast! The problem is it's hardest when you're first beginning to defeat self-doubt, which is why most people don't. They give up before they even get going because they doubt themselves and their abilities.

You have to trust the process. That is the best way to defeat self-doubt. Once you start building momentum, the rest is history.

Transcending and evolving is when you pull the strings in your daily life, and your self-doubt and your lazy mind become the consistent, obedient loser to your conscious mind. Instead of being a slave to your bad habits, you become master of them.

I've gotten good at fighting my lazy mind. When I wake up in the morning, my lazy mind complains and moans. It wants to fight and go back to sleep, but my conscious mind knows I should get up and go to the gym.

When I get to the gym, my lazy mind complains and moans that it doesn't feel like working out. When my lazy mind puts its fists up, my conscious mind grabs a bazooka and blows it out of the water. Your mind is a muscle. The more you exercise and feed that muscle memory of your conscious mind succeeding over your lazy mind, the easier it becomes.

Initially, I was so scared to start my business that I would wake up and think about getting out of bed. I'd lie to myself about the benefits of staying asleep. I'd say things like, "Oh, if I sleep in, I'll be more focused, alert, and ready to really concentrate on work."

I denied the responsibility to improve my life. I'd say to myself, "It doesn't even matter if I did get up, what change would one day at the gym make?"

So, I would go back to sleep. Later in the day, I'd regret it. To make myself feel better, I'd promise myself that was the last time.

I would also start the work day knowing I needed to make sales and bring value and money into my business so I could reinvest in more automation and scale. Unfortunately, I would lie to myself and say, "It's okay to not sell today," and just read some blogs, watch some YouTube videos, and deny all responsibility for my financial and business situation. Then I'd regret my decision and promise myself tomorrow was the day. Only to repeat it all over again.

When you have the introspective and self-reflective ability required to recognize the difference between your lazy mind and your conscious mind, everything changes. I learned to observe my lazy mind for what it was and recognize when it appeared. I learned the pattern.

My lazy mind, and the habits associated with it, had become so strong that it had me totally under its control. It was constantly dragging me down and distracting me from what I knew I needed to do to reach my dreams.

I learned to fight my lazy mind. I learned to overpower it. I learned to win the battle against myself and the bad habits ingrained in my daily life. I learned my patterns, and I took control and evolved into the next, better version of myself, because becoming is better than being.

Love and Hate

I like to perform an exercise in which I define my dreams, and then tell as many people as possible. I call them accountability partners. Being successful is hard—it's so much easier to give up.

I always say you need true love or true hate to make it as an entrepreneur. True love for your family or kids, or true hate for your boss or your current life to make it through all the roadblocks, bumps, blood, sweat, and tears required to build something meaningful and life-changing.

Human beings will do more to not embarrass themselves in front of other people than they will to improve themselves. You really have to have the pressure to succeed, from external parties, your family, your wife, husband, or friends; the more people you tell about your dreams, the BETTER!

You want to define your dream. Make it as vivid as possible. Where do you want to live? What do you want to do during the day?

Now, tell your exact dreams in as vivid detail as possible to everyone who will listen, your family, friends, and co-workers. Even if they don't care or only pretend to care, you're not doing it for them, you're doing it to HOLD YOURSELF accountable! The more you tell other people and get them involved in it, the more pressure you put on yourself to perform.

Chapter 33

Change Your Habits,
Change Your Life

"It's kind of fun to do the impossible."
— Walt Disney

We all know habits are the foundation for success, but how do you actually change your habits? This is probably the most important thing you could possibly learn to expedite your path to success. The only difference between millionaires and non-millionaires is consistent daily habits exponentiated over time through compound interest.

When you take most people who are hard-wired to procrastinate, it takes some real effort to get them to take action. When I first started making my first course, establishing proof of concept, and recording YouTube videos, my brain would scream to do anything other than what I knew I needed to do.

I knew that the highest value activity I could do was to add forty targeted people from relevant Facebook groups, message them, and add them to my group. I knew the highest value thing I could do was consistently make proven YouTube video topics.

How I Hacked It

When I woke up each morning, I knew the first thing I needed to do was get to my computer, ready to work. So the only thing I would concentrate on was showering and getting to my computer, dressed and ready to go.

I wouldn't think about all the things I needed to do or videos I needed to make. I would only think about getting dressed and in front of my computer; that was step #1.

My lazy mind would make every excuse. "Kevin, you're already successful…it's cold…let's just sleep a little longer and you'll be more rested…let's browse Reddit just to wake up…"

It's really shocking how good the human mind is at rationalizing stagnation. It is critical to become self-aware and spot when your lazy mind attempts to overpower you and take back control.

As another trick, use what is called "basic animalistic reward psychology."

The human brain, similar to an animal's, operates on a reward basis. Do a task or something you know is necessary, then you reward yourself. You'll start to associate the completion of a task with the pleasure you receive for the reward.

For example, when I finished creating my YouTube video, a Facebook post, or reaching out and adding forty targeted people on Facebook and messaging them, I would play thirty minutes of Xbox, which was my reset and reward time.

If your trigger is waking up at 8 am, and your high-value actions are sending out forty targeted friend requests and messages on Facebook and recording one proven YouTube video from start to finish, then your reward could be thirty minutes or an hour of Xbox, reading, Yoga, or ice cream; it doesn't matter what it is. You can hack your mind into associating that hard work with the reward you give yourself after you're done.

The most critical habit of all is focus.

A strategy I like to use for focusing is a simple one. I've tried all types of things, from natural supplements to apps, and the simplest one works best for me. I use a countdown timer and set an alarm for one hour. Set the timer, turn your phone on airplane mode, put it in a drawer, out of your vision, sit somewhere clean and tidy, and start the timer with absolutely no distractions. This is what is called deep work, devoid of all distractions. You want to have time to think clearly and get into deep work because that is when the magic happens.

Try it, and see how many times your lazy mind tries to reach for your phone, or brings it to the front of your mind. It's a strange thing to be self-aware of. Your mind will also rationalize why it reached for the phone. "Oh, just one last reminder", or "I forgot to send that email/message!"

I promise even though at first you'll be yearning for your phone, because that habit has formed in your mind, soon you'll be in the zone. This is what deep work creates.

It is like meditation; it takes time and consistent effort, and is like a muscle that must be trained with repetition.

Another favorite focus and productivity tip I've learned over the years is to only focus on one task per day, never more than one. If you have to establish proof of concept, do only that and focus on setting up consultations. If you have to set up your Facebook groups, do only that. Constantly bouncing around between different tasks kills your overall productivity.

Be Passionate

Learn to fall in love with learning new things, technology, and your work, because these are the things average people hate. How many times have you heard someone complain about technology, procrastinate on learning something new, or dread going to work?

Most people are so obsessed with the money they don't even enjoy the work. All they can think about is money. It's a toxic cycle, because even when they reach the goal, they've habituated that unquenchable thirst for more and more and can't even enjoy it. I'm friends with a lot of very wealthy people who don't enjoy their wealth at all.

Michael Jordan was was for becoming the best basketball player because of his love of the game. His love of the game motivated him to practice all of time. Any spare moment would go into improving his game.

This is how I feel with digital course creation, online marketing, and content creation. There is always something new to learn—it is FUN. It is a puzzle I love solving, it's mentally stimulating, and I honestly enjoy it!

With enough consistent, intention-focused, directional, daily effort, you become the best in the world. No one becomes the best at what they do without falling in love with the work. An added bonus is that you're just going to be a happier person if you enjoy the process rather than relentlessly grinding toward the goal.

Time passes whether you enjoy it or not. So, make it your goal to fall in love with the work you're doing, learn to love learning itself, love your clients, your customers, and your students. Love it all because if you don't, you're not going to do anything special.

No Zero Days

Always ground yourself in the present. Don't plan things days, weeks, or months in advance. You know what adds the most value to your business. If you need a reminder, it's reaching out to potential customers, building your Facebook group, and making proven YouTube content.

You won't always feel like maintaining your momentum. Sometimes you won't feel like doing anything, but on those days it's critical to ask yourself, "What is the one thing I can do today that will give me even the tiniest amount of momentum?" That's what you want to focus on.

No zero days is a concept I developed for myself years ago. When I didn't feel like working out, I would tell myself okay do just one push up, literally one. Once I got over the mental barrier of doing anything at all, I would do one push up, and then I would do 49 more because I had broken that initial mental blockade.

It's the same with focus and business. You have to do something each day, break the mental barrier, even if it's adding one person and sending one message, or researching YouTube videos; just start. You'll often find that once you do, it gets easier to keep on going.

📖 Part 4 Summary

- You learned how to use pre-existing resources to expedite the process needed to create a chronological, well-thought-out skeleton for your course.
- You learned about creating a skeleton for your course in the form of Chapters and Parts, and to outline your course following the Grandma Principle, or in such a simple way that even your dear old grandma would understand.
- You learned about using Idea Branding to liven up your course, make your chapter and sections more memorable, and credited to you when people discuss them.
- You learned about how to incentivize your students to participate in your private group and how vital this is for success and community building.
- You learned about how to price your course for explosive sales and the strategy behind pricing to be the premium option in your market niche.
- You learned about the lazy mind vs. the conscious mind, how to hack your brain to control those split-second decisions to be lazy or productive, and how they exponentiate over time!
- You learned about the necessary mentality for success, and how accountability partners help you achieve your dreams.
- You learned about the critical nature of focus, the finite nature of mental energy, and my strategies for achieving focus.

☑ Part 4 Checklist

- Have you found and analyzed the chronological structure of similar courses, and looked for proven patterns of organization for your topic?
- Have you created your skeleton in the form of a table of contents with your chapter titles and a rough outline of the content in each chapter?
- Have you idea branded the information inside your course to be more memorable?
- Have you incentivized and made it easy to participate in your Private Facebook group, and incentivized throughout your course information to have students share their success stories?
- Have you analyzed your competition, reviewed the pricing, and set your price as the premium brand in your niche?

If you're committed and ready for more, go to www.digitalcoursesecrets.com/go to learn about how to access example chapters from my Facebook Ads Masterclass and additional recommended course creation tools.

Part 5
Technological Evolution

Chapter 34

Becoming the Master

"If I had an hour to solve a problem, I'd spend 55 minutes thinking about the problem and 5 minutes thinking about solutions."
— Albert Einstein

Technology is the ultimate equalizer. Until recently, if you wanted to grow a large scale business, you had to have a large office and a huge number of employees. There was a massive amount of overhead and headache involved with being an entrepreneur.

That still happens every day. People work extremely hard creating construction businesses, restaurants, or any number of businesses requiring a ton of work and dealing with illogical and emotional human capital (employees).

You're smarter than that. You understand the knowledge economy and that by leveraging technology you can grow a 6, 7 or even 8-Figure business with few employees or upfront capital/overhead. To grow my business to $10,000,000 in sales in under two years from zero, in recent history, I would have needed hundreds if not thousands of employees. Leveraging technology the right way, I was able to do it with just myself and a few virtual assistants!

The internet is a beautiful thing. It allows a single person to create a massive business, but it is not possible to do so without an understanding and love for the technology involved. It is critical you shift your mindset from hating technology, and falsely thinking you're bad at it, to loving it.

Technology allows anyone, with enough effort, to create a multi-million dollar business with close to zero employees. At no other time in history has it been possible to create a massively scaled business with so few employees as you now can by leveraging automation and technology. It is truly magical. The sooner you learn to love the benefits technology provides instead of dreading it, the sooner you'll become more successful than your wildest dreams!

Generally in business, to get more profits requires more production, sales, and customers, which in turn, requires more employees, infrastructure, and bureaucracy. This means more exhaustion, oversight, and work time for you, which means less comfort, autonomy, and free time. It defeats the entire purpose of becoming an entrepreneur—financial and temporal freedom.

In the "old model" of business, if you wanted more profits, it meant a bigger office, more employees, the works! The knowledge economy has changed that because, with technology, you eliminate the need for additional employees. You are able to build a massive business if you leverage your automated infrastructure correctly.

If you have been conditioned to dread technology, to hate it, or to think you are not good at it, then it is time to make an intentional shift of your mindset. You're no longer someone who "doesn't know." You now have the GIN mentality and realize the answer to almost any technological issue is just one Google search, YouTube search, or support chat conversation away.

Einstein said, "Never memorize something that you can look up," and those words are truer now more than ever! You have the world's information at your fingertips. Use it when you get stuck.

When I was an accountant, we had ten different spreadsheets we used in our day-to-day jobs, and we needed to take samples to ensure that specific people in the companies we were auditing had taken specific safety quizzes. We had to look at the employee registration spreadsheet, which had only employee numbers. We had to find the employee names by cross-referencing their numbers in a separate spreadsheet, and then we had to compare the name in another spreadsheet documenting who had completed the safety quiz. Then I had to summarize all these different data points one by one into yet another spreadsheet.

This is how everyone did it. I remember thinking, *there has to be a better way*. I was researching and trying to figure things out, and my co-workers were laughing at me saying how they had completed twenty different samples, and I hadn't finished any because I was looking for a more efficient way to do things.

After a few hours, I had reverse engineered an Excel script entirely from Google searching to do 100% of the work for me. By the time I finished, my co-workers had finished eighty samples in the four hours it took me to reverse engineer the Excel script.

Once I was done setting up the Excel script and executing it, in seconds, I had completed all one hundred of my required samples while my co-workers had only finished eighty, even though for the first four hours, I had completed zero samples. That is the power of technology—spending more time now to spend infinitely less time in the future.

As you grow your business and it becomes more difficult to know what to spend your time on, always err on the side of technology and setting up the infrastructure for automation.

When you do it once, it's done forever. It works silently in the night as your unstoppable workforce, never making errors or mistakes, or taking sick days. It's an inexhaustible machine that does exactly what you set it up to do.

Remember everything in this next section is the culmination of 10,000 hours of hard work, trial and error, failure, blood, sweat, tears, and thousands of dollars wasted on software, split testing funnels, landing pages, pop-ups, copy, and everything technologically required to make a masterpiece course.

The best part for you is the result of all my wasted time, effort, and energy is packaged and bundled up perfectly to skip years of mistakes and jump directly into the most effective and cost-efficient services you need to be successful!

The Ecosystem

I want to quickly introduce the two or three funnels every successful course needs, and the reason I say 2 OR 3 is because if you intend to sell a product for $497 or higher, you also need a webinar funnel. If you intend to sell a cheaper product, then you do not need a webinar funnel.

Funnel #1—Your Sales Funnel

Every funnel should have at least three steps:

- **The Sales Page:** Where people learn more about who you are and what you sell—generally colder traffic
- **The Order Page:** Where people purchase your course and you deliver testimonials and results—generally warmer traffic
- **The Thank You Page:** Where people go after they purchase. This is one of the places you deliver membership info and install your purchase event pixels, which we will discuss in the next part.

Funnel #2—Your Membership Funnel

Your membership funnel is where people login with their purchase email. Their access will be automatically assigned when they purchase access to a series of videos you will record, host on Vimeo or a free option like YouTube, and then embed on your membership funnel!

Funnel #3—Your Webinar Funnel (For Courses Above $497)

My webinars have made me millions of dollars while I sleep as a never-ending workforce spreading my message every second of every minute of every day, without any direct input required.

Webinars are also daunting technologically for most people because the technology required to create a webinar that plays every fifteen minutes all day every day is no easy task.

Most people starting out have what I like to call the "little doubter voice" in the back of their head that says, "No one will ever pay me $497 or $997 for a course I make based on knowledge in my head. That is CRAZY!"

I had it when I started, and I would argue every successful course creator has it when they start. It is incredibly important to acknowledge the little doubter voice and destroy it from the start. I still see creators with huge followings afraid to charge what they're worth, and it's costing them millions!

I have had over 10,000 people invest in my courses, most of which were for $997-$1997 or more! This stuff works. You won't believe it until you experience it, but trust the process until you do, and you'll thank me later.

Your webinar is your workhorse. If you intend to sell a course for $497 or higher, you can make it more valuable with one-on-one calls or your personal attention.

Maybe I start out selling an A-Z walkthrough of selling on Amazon in PDF format for $47. I'm collecting emails, building rapport, and delivering value, getting people into my email ecosystem and Facebook groups. I pixel them for later retargeting, and then I decide to sell a done-for-you PPC for Amazon service for $197.

Maybe a few months later, I decide to build a full-fledged Amazon FBA A-Z course and offer it for $997. I can guarantee a large percentage of the initial buyers of my lower ticket offers will join my higher ticket course!

If you intend to jump immediately into a $497 or higher ticket offer (which you absolutely should!), then you need to have a webinar. You webinar funnel operates as what is commonly referred to as a "JIT" or Just in Time.

What this essentially means is that every 15 minutes, your webinar will always be starting "Just in Time." If someone hits your page at 3:05 pm, the website will show there is another webinar starting in 10 minutes, or if they arrive at 3:14 pm, the website will show another webinar starting in 1 minute! It is always just in time!

Your webinar transforms cold audiences into believers in you, with a formulaic, battle-tested presentation.

- First, edifying you as someone worth listening to.
- Then enticing your viewers to stay throughout the presentation.
- Then teaching them just enough for them to understand how amazing your opportunity is.
- Then using time-based scarcity and fear of missing out on your bonuses to close them right then and there.

The below chart is the best summary of the flow of an excellent webinar. A webinar is a presentation specifically designed to always be available to view and learn from. Ideally, viewers will make a purchase because of it!

It begins with grabbing attention, then you build rapport, introduce yourself, and gain credibility. You want to agitate their pain and target their problems; what is it they want to fix with this webinar? Show the benefits only you provide, then lather on the social proof that shows your methods are the best. Set expectations to keep them grounded, then show them your solution, which outshines their expectations. Hit them with the offer they can't resist, remove the risk with a money back guarantee, and give them a hard deadline to make a decision!

This may seem overwhelming, but you just need to recognize and understand the basic elements.

You need to make your webinar viewers feel that going with you is the lowest risk choice.

You need to make your webinar viewers feel like they would miss out on the deal of a lifetime by doing anything OTHER than buy from you!

Remember, people have bought courses from people with significantly lower moral standards than YOURS—so you need to make them understand you are different, and you really care!

You do that in a number of very specific ways…

You want your webinar to teach but **NOT TEACH TOO MUCH.** You want to teach just enough to give them an "Aha" moment where they think, "Wow, this does look possible!"

You will inevitably have people who joined your free webinar expecting you to drop everything and teach them one-on-one for the rest of your life for free; don't focus on these people.

It's important to understand how the webinar works, but **it's more important to just get it done**. Trust me. Trust the people who have dedicated their lives to mastering sales presentations. Trust the proof of hundreds of millions of dollars worth of products sold using these strategies. You are a doer now, so do!

Chapter 35

From Stranger to Buyer:
The Art of the Sales Funnel

A sales funnel is designed to convert someone who knows nothing about you, or has loosely heard about you from a friend, an advertisement, or YouTube video, and turn them into a buyer!

The Sales Page (Inside the Sales Funnel)

If you've ever tried to meet someone new at a bar or club, at the start, you would be considered "cold traffic" to one another. I like to think about the sales page as a slightly more targeted night at the bar.

Once you see a beautiful man or woman, you warm up a bit and show a fleeting moment of interest and desire to learn more. This is the art of the sales page. You want to think of your sales page as the first conversation at a bar, but the problem is it's not a normal conversation, it's a one-way conversation!

This means you need to be very precise and deliberate with what information you use to communicate, to turn someone who was previously a "cold audience," or someone who's never heard of you, into someone who might potentially be interested in what you have to say. Think about your sales page as a way to make them curious, agitate their pain or fears, and present yourself as the most logical, genuine vehicle to their desires.

The four red X's in the image below represent the four BIGGEST FEARS, WORRIES AND FRUSTRATIONS I heard again and again from the people I initially offered free 15-minute phone calls to do market research. This stuff is all sequential; it's all a chronological timeline. Each step has a purpose, and as you learn these things, you start to become unbelievably valuable to the market as a consultant, to your students, to other business owners. People see a frustration similar to their own, and they think, "Oh gosh, that's me!" It keeps them reading.

Understanding how to create the full structure and ecosystem for a digital course, or selling any type of product is absolutely INVALUABLE!

The sales page presented features a prominent smiling person. Humans react to other smiling humans instinctively.

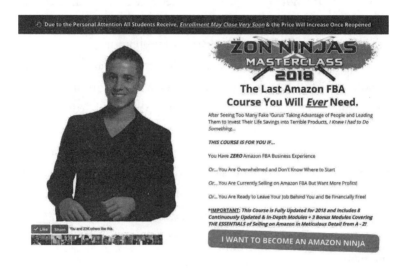

Location Game Theory

If you're creating a course that currently has other popular courses, there will be sales copy somewhere else. If there is not, take sales copy from me, or someone you know is successful, even if it is about a totally different subject. Reverse engineer it!

You can have the number one proven, successful course open in a second window while you're writing your sales page. It would be silly not to use it as inspiration; it's proven it works!

Find something proven, read their sales page, review one line at a time, and reverse engineer it to be relevant for your course topic, while making improvements based on your market research!

For the people who are worried that if they make a course similar to another popular course, it will hurt the course creator: it's actually the opposite because of what is called "location game theory."

Have you ever considered why multiple fast food restaurants are often near one another, or why there are gas stations or hotels near each other? It's not by chance. It creates a centralized district that attracts consumers to the businesses (or ideas) as a whole, when otherwise, they would not have ever known about it.

Clustering businesses also adds competition and alternative options, which demands the quality of each offering to increase, or else a single competitor would dominate (if they had the highest quality).

It also benefits the new entry to the market, as people have already heard about the offering, and have become accustomed to the idea of paying to learn the subject matter. If someone has heard of the course topic, you've already won half the battle! It's twice as much work explaining what your course is, and then selling someone into your program.

Often times, people think you coming in as new competition to the incumbent course creators is bad for them, but it's actually better for them. You are actually helping your competition, and vice versa. The consumer likes having options, and if you excel in customer support and have a great course, you will win!

📖 Part 5 Summary

- You learned about the transition from novice to master, and the understanding required to navigate the complexity that comes with creating a massively successful business!
- You learned about the sales funnel and how each sequential step is designed to continue your customer onward down your funnel to your desired final destination.
- You reviewed the importance of never reinventing the wheel and using proven sales copy from similar courses or proven successful people to emulate for your own course.

✅ Part 5 Checklist

- Do you have a basic understanding of how a Sales Funnel works?
- Have you thoroughly researched and notated the most popular and proven sales page copy in your course topic niche?
- Have you set up your Membership funnel?
- Have you learned how to use the secret sign up URL for your membership funnel?

There are so many amazing things you can do with funnels, but some things just can't be accurately portrayed as text in a book.
Click on the link below to learn more about getting:

- Multi-million dollar pre-built webinars, sales funnels, and membership funnels
- Instructions to set up your domain and support email

- Support in setting up your million dollar sales funnel
- Example privacy policy, terms of service, and earnings disclaimers
- Guidance on how to create your own onboarding emails

To get my Free 8-Figure funnel ecosystem, check out my free training—open your internet browser and type in www.digitalcoursesecrets.com/go right now!

Part 6

Marketing Mastery

Chapter 36
The Art of Storytelling

"Marketing is no longer about the stuff that you make,
but about the story you tell."
— Seth Godin

M arketing is the driving force behind your success. Your course is the yin, and marketing is the yang of making your movement a reality. For marketing to work, you must have a product worth marketing, and for your course to take off, you must have marketing good enough for people to be interested in giving it a chance!

The goal of paid traffic is to get people to register for your webinar or download your cheatsheet. With your cheatsheet and entirely free organic traffic, you could just set it up. When people downloaded it, it was free. Everything was great because they were coming from YouTube or your Facebook group and didn't cost you a dime. Now, you're going to be paying to get people to join your ecosystem and download your cheatsheet, watch your webinar, or give you their email address.

Mindset Matters

To be successful and start making more money than you could have ever possibly imagined, you have to believe you can do it and that you deserve it.

Mastering your psychology is critical to finding long term success and fulfillment. Legendary psychologist Sir David Hawkins said that, "People simply mirror back [their] internal belief systems." Success begins with believing you will do what you say you will. Believing what you say begins with your actions. Following through on actions creates confidence, and nothing breeds confidence like having confidence. It is a positive feedback loop that creates a snowball effect.

It can quickly spiral the other way if you aren't in direct control of your psychology. You need to confront "Imposter Syndrome" head-on, because it is very real and affects ALL humans.

Imposter Syndrome versus Confident Expert

Impostor Syndrome is a proven psychological pattern in which an individual doubts their accomplishments and has a persistent internalized fear of being exposed as a "fraud." It's unbelievable how imposter syndrome affects us.

Experts are only experts because they care more about learning subjects than anyone else. Confidence is key when it comes to getting people to believe in themselves enough to take action! You don't have to be a world-class expert to help people either, you just have to be one step ahead of those you help, and you have to genuinely do the work to become an expert by caring more and doing daily research!

Believing and knowing you deserve success as much as anyone else is half the battle to getting the life you want, so you have to act the part, believe you deserve it, and invest in creating your dream.

Remember, every expert starts as a beginner. I can guarantee you that when LeBron James wakes up each morning, he BELIEVES he deserves what he has. I can guarantee you that before he had it, he believed he deserved it and knew it was coming.

Consistent, smart work has a funny way of doing that. Unwavering confidence creates a chain reaction of positive effects in your life. Successful people believe they deserve the things they've worked hard to achieve.

People give you what YOU BELIEVE you deserve. People naturally reflect back toward you what you believe about yourself. Each day you sincerely work hard and trust the process of what you've learned, you'll start to accumulate meaningful wins, like new members in your Facebook group and a few people watching your YouTube videos. Then a few more will join until you reach the moment your incremental efforts and compound interest explode, giving you exponential returns for your efforts!

If you don't believe you deserve it, no one else will. If you really work harder learning, researching, becoming the best, and simply CARE MORE, your confidence will grow daily, and you will become an expert. If you believe you deserve it, and you believe in yourself, others will follow suit, but it starts with you.

Your Story

I have interviewed many people who buy my courses and ask them where they heard about me and why they joined my program rather than one of my competitors'. Most people assume the main reason people buy my programs is because the content is superior or because of the price, but literally zero people have ever given those reasons.

People buy because they trust you, because you're genuine, and because of your STORY!

You want to develop your story from the beginning and be genuine with it. The closer your story hits home with your target audience, the more explosive your course sales will be!

All of what you say online and via video is permanent, which is one reason always telling the truth is so critical. It's too hard to remember white lies, so you don't even want to consider it, regardless of what other people are doing. Being honest will always serve you in the long run.

You want to formulate your story in a very specific way and get used to saying it often. It's okay to repeat yourself in the content you create, because people may only watch one out of ten of your YouTube videos, or one of five of your Facebook group posts, or perhaps see you once on Instagram or a podcast.

Never worry you're saying it too much. Remember that potential customers are ALL experiencing more or less the same thing. They have a surface goal, such as wanting to make more money, and a goal below the surface, such as wanting their family to respect them and be proud of them.

The most important transition is from WANT to HAD. For example, "I realized I didn't just want to earn more money. I realized if I wanted to put food on the table, and prevent my kids from starving, I HAD to do something."

Remember: you want to directly associate and be relatable with as many of your targeted potential customers as possible. This means there are two extremely important points to master here.

You want your backstory or timeline to be close to the exact same place where your target audience is right now, because they want what you have proven is possible to get, and more importantly, possible for them to get!

This means your one MOMENT that everything changed needs

to line up as close to where they're at now as possible. For example:

"I was struggling badly, living paycheck to paycheck when I finally stumbled on selling on Amazon completely by chance while watching YouTube videos. I got an eviction notice in the mail and only had 72 hours to move myself, my wife, and kids out. We had nowhere to go unless we came up with the final $500. I didn't sleep for one minute of that 72 hours and ended up making just over $1,000 in those three days selling stuff from around the house, which paid for our rent for the next month. That is when my life completely changed…"

This is relatable because maybe they learn from YouTube videos as well, maybe they live paycheck to paycheck, and it appeals to their emotions because you were close to eviction and made it happen with your back against the wall. If they see where you once were and it is where they're at now, they will have faith they can do it too!

You want your followers to think three important things:

1. "Wow, that person seems genuine!"
2. "Wow, I can really relate to that person!"
3. "Wow, that person's message really hit me!"

If you can accomplish these three things, course sales will never be a problem for you.

Make it real, make it a story, illustrate it, make them FEEL it! When you're genuine, and they FEEL IT, you win. People have incredibly fine-tuned BS meters nowadays, so you can't fake this. It has to be real. It has to be honest.

Remember: true excellence is intoxicating, and in a world where most people don't care about the little things, you can stand out even with incrementally more tender loving care than your competitors.

Marketing is about the angles by which you portray information.

You should never lie, but you always want to show the aspects of a situation you want people to see.

So be genuine. Tell your story, be relatable, remember where you were, and describe the details down to the watercooler talk in your cubicle. Describe the real human parts of the pain they're experiencing and give them a way out. You did it, and you are now their vehicle for massive change!

I was a 9-5 drone making $55k a year, and now I've made over $10 million in 18 months from nothing!

You might not have a story like that yet. Here's the thing nobody knows or can understand. I created my story from my cubicle 18 months ago, entirely in my head. I didn't know exactly when it would happen or how down to the last detail, but I knew it would happen. I wrote my history before it happened—I knew I wasn't destined for the 9-5 life. I knew I was destined for more. I took everything bad about my past life, and rewrote it as something I was thankful for and learned from, and I came out stronger.

A lot of people drift through life thinking the perfect time to start is going to magically appear, but the reality is you'll be waiting your whole life, and it won't happen; there is no such thing as the perfect time to start. The best time to start was twenty years ago; the second best time is today. You reading these words right now means you're 95% of the way there, because getting started is the hardest part!

You have to INTERVENE in your life. There is no perfect time. It starts with changing your beliefs, because when you believe something, you'll take action in accordance with those beliefs. When you have a belief, you take action, you get results, and you gain confidence from those results, which feeds your belief and thus your actions!

Chapter 37
Specific, Sequential Steps

"The best marketing doesn't feel like marketing."
— Tom Fishburne

A successful course launch begins months before the launch actually occurs. People think a course creator suddenly decides to launch his or her course, and it becomes a massive success. This is simply not true.

The launch period only works, and marketing in general works, because of the core infrastructure presented in prior parts of *Unfair Advantage*. If you don't choose an evergreen proven course, when you go to get proof of concept and create your minimum viable product, it won't work correctly. Think of creating a course as building blocks. Without each block, the entire structure would fall.

Each step is sequential:

1. Choosing your evergreen course topic
2. Giving massive free value in your Facebook group and YouTube videos
3. Establishing proof of concept via free + paid done-for-you solutions/consultations

4. Building your course content in the form of outlines + videos in your membership area

5. Building your course tech in the form of sales, webinar, and membership funnels

ONLY then can you market correctly. Without completing each prior step, the process fails. You must devote your entire mental energy to one or the other—you CANNOT do both at the same time!

By the time you're ready to launch your course, you've filmed a double-digit number of YouTube videos and helped every single member in your group with every single one of their questions. Because of that, when you go to release your course and open it for enrollment, you'll get people saying, "You gave away such amazing content completely for free, I HAD to see what was in your course!"

Be Specific

Have your offer be VERY SPECIFIC in your marketing. Most beginners make the fatal mistake of being general in their marketing to try to appeal to more people. This is not how sales work!

If someone sees an ad for a cheatsheet on advertising, versus seeing an ad for a cheatsheet for the top 7 things that college students who live in Portland, Oregon need to know to get a job in advertising in 30 days or less, which are they going to choose?

Beginners think that by offering more options they will make more sales by catering to more people's potential desires. This could not be further from the truth!

Make your offer simple, to the point, and singularly focused. If you're selling an Amazon FBA course, sell an Amazon FBA course and that is all. Don't try to package it together with other forms of eCom. It simply doesn't work.

Don't make an Amazon, Shopify, Affiliate marketing monstrosity. Stick to one thing you've proven and market to those people as SPECIFICALLY as you possibly can, because someone is much more likely to take action with an offer more specifically catered to them.

Any amount of money for a product people don't understand is TOO much! If you try to market your course as the one-stop-shop for starting a business, no one will buy because it doesn't make sense. There are thousands of different types of businesses and ways to make money online.

You MUST be specific, niche down, and become a specialist. You, as the creator, have to actively and thoughtfully manage people and prevent them from being overwhelmed. Remember that EMOTION makes sales, not logic. You want the person to picture how much better their life will be in the future if they join your course and implement what you teach.

You need to connect with people. If you make things emotional, you will sell 100x more. With a higher ticket purchase, normally both wife/husband or family are involved, and they have to believe you can help better their lives. The rapport you've built by giving away content for free and communicating via video helps IMMEASURABLY here!

You need to make it blatantly obvious that the old way (their current mindset) and the new way are arch enemies, and the only way to defeat that old, status quo evil cubicle is with YOU!

By this point, you would have validated your course idea through three or more paid consultations, you should have some email sign-ups and even beta students, if you chose to select a few of them who wanted to join before your course was even finished because they believe in you and the value you provide.

Every day, you've been adding 40 new Facebook friends. Every day, you've been private messaging everybody who accepts your friend request on Facebook or LinkedIn. Every day you're posting in your Facebook group and on your Facebook page. Every week, you're emailing your list (even if it's one person!) with an update, or a case study, success story, a piece of content, or an offer!

Next, host a live training in your Facebook group or on YouTube, giving massive value twice per month. These can be motivational, value-added, tutorials, YouTube videos, other people's articles you find interesting—anything helpful!

Finally, ask your existing students/clients for testimonials in the form of Facebook comments and short, to-the-point videos, and post them as content monthly or weekly if possible!

When I first created my Facebook group, I had this big build up, and I thought I was going to have the biggest launch ever. I triple-checked my post announcing my course, and I pressed submit. I was so nervous. I was waiting for people to flood in and buy my course!

The post I wrote talked about the course itself and how revolutionary it was, how it was going to change people's lives, what you would get and all the value; it was an amazing summary of the course itself. I thought it was great!

And no one responded, not one person. I was devastated.

But I had an *Unfair Advantage*…

I recognized failure doesn't exist, only feedback…

So, the next day I tried something different. I took one of my beta students and showed a screenshot they posted in my private group showing how they went from $0 to $10,000 in sales on Amazon from scratch!

I didn't even say I had a course. I didn't mention anything about selling it, and I got a TON of comments from people in my larger public group asking where they could get more info, how they could join my course, and where they could sign up!

This is an important point because people don't care about you or your course, and that's okay! They care about themselves and how your course can get them what they desire, or help them leave their pain behind!

Your Facebook page has been set up, your personal Facebook has been cleaned up and made professional, and your LinkedIn as well. Everything you've done has been for a purpose, and that is because when someone hears about you, they do research and due diligence.

When you've started to drop all these bread crumbs all over the place, like testimonials, and content posts, and when people stumble across your online presence and your success stories, it creates a compelling story. It's like laying bait to bring people back to you.

Chapter 38

The Remix to Ignition:
Steps to a Perfect Launch

The purpose of a launch is to transition your followers, the people who've until now been on the receiving end of a massive amount of free value, into actual buyers of your course. This is where the incremental compound interest you've been building for the past months pays off immensely. The more people you've added value to up until this point, the easier and more explosive this process will be!

The Arch Enemy of the Launch

Our main enemy will be human nature. Humans want to push off big decisions. This is a big reason most people remain average.

You'll find being decisive is commonality most successful people share. The ability to make decisions (even large ones) quickly and confidently. Have you ever had a friend who could never decide on where to eat lunch to save their life? Have you ever had a friend or family member who always seemed to know what they were doing and where they were going? Did you have more confidence in the one who struggled to make a decision or the one who was more decisive?

The decisive trait is not shared by most people, so it will be your job to use a variety of marketing techniques to help overcome your potential customers' natural inclinations to procrastinate the decision to join your course!

The 3 most powerful marketing tools in your toolbelt are:

- Curiosity
- Scarcity
- Exclusivity

No one can resist the NEW revelation, the newest best diet, the one secret to the love life of their dreams, or the BEST new way to make money online. If people believe they are going to miss out on something, it is the SINGLE most powerful reason behind a purchase decision.

You are going to use these tools to get people to take the final step and join your program. If your program is going to make them more money than it costs, or if it is going to make them feel better than they ever have before, or finds them the love of their life, then it would be SELFISH of you not to do anything you can to get them to join!

When you honestly believe your course is worth more than the money it costs, selling is no longer selling, it's helping people create the change they desire. You become the vehicle that helps them make the changes they need!

I used to feel guilty charging $997 for my courses until people went on to make hundreds of thousands of dollars from my teachings and became millionaires. If someone giving you $1,000 can turn into $1,000,000, should you feel guilty charging them the $1,000, or should you feel guilty *not doing everything you can* to get them to turn that $1,000 into a million?

Luckily, you have some incredible weapons in your arsenal of helping people take massive action!

The Big Four of Marketing

1. **Reward Fast Action:** "For the first ten people who join, we are going to be taking 50% off the normal price."
2. **Exclusivity:** "We are only accepting ten people into the course to ensure we have time and bandwidth to work with each person one-on-one to help ensure their success!"
3. **Scarcity:** "We are shutting down this opportunity Sunday at 11:59 pm, so if you don't want to miss out forever, join now; it's your last chance!"
4. **Curiosity:** "Learn the little known, simple strategy I used to sell $30,000 of everyday products from around the house on Amazon in my first month!"

Only ever use techniques in your marketing that are true. It always pays off, in the long run, to be honest. Really do take 50% off for the first ten people, really do only accept ten people to start for a while before you reopen the course, and close down the ability to join for a time at 11:59 pm on Sunday!

I've tried both ways, and when I used none of these tactics, guess what happened? No one bought. Think about Walmart. Obviously, they could just charge what it actually costs them plus a reasonable profit margin for all of their products—yet they still use sales and clearance. Use what works.

Use these strategies on Facebook posts, groups, emails, the content of YouTube videos, EVERYWHERE! Remember these steps are important to understand and start to implement into your emails, the way you speak, your Facebook posts, and all your communication mediums.

Launching

Step #1: Agitate Their Current Situation (Pain)

In the first stage of your launch content, you need to remind people of their current situation. Describe the problems they're dealing with and the pain they're experiencing.

It seems negative, I know.

Remember, you need to address the pain your audience is experiencing to show them you understand and to incentivize them to take action.

This helps build trust and puts them in the mindset where you become the obvious solution to their current pain!

"The one big mistake when it comes to Amazon…"

"Why you just can't get your butt to the gym, it takes more than that…"

"What Everybody Needs to Know Before Buying Their First House"

"What to never, ever say during a job interview…"

Step #2: Future Place Where They COULD Be (Pleasure)

Talking about the benefits AFTER agitating their pain creates a stark CONTRAST to the pain you described in Step 1.

This awakens your customers desire to get to pleasure. It makes people realize they want what you're selling BEFORE you even make your offer!

Now, in this second stage, you should also offer some INSPIRATION. Let people know—or better yet, SHOW them—that it's possible. The best way to do this is with a story or case study of someone who managed to move away from their pain and achieve pleasure. This could be a personal story about you, or it could be about a client or someone else you've helped.

Your three testimonials, screenshots that show sales, or video testimonials about how your course changed their lives and took them from their PAIN to their DESIRED result come in handy here!

Step #3: Present the Obvious Answer (Solution)

In Step 3, you need to show your customers that a solution is not only possible but that YOU have the RIGHT and ONLY solution for them.

This means that you need to get practical and deliver a technique, an insight, or a useful resource that helps your ideal customers achieve a SMALL WIN.

This is crucial because people need to feel a sense of accomplishment. They need to feel that they're already moving closer to the pleasure. And they need to believe that you're the person to take them there.

Step #4: Remove Friction by Addressing ALL Reservations (Objection Handling)

Now it's the time to address some of the common fears and objections that hold people back. You want to become a MASTER at eliminating all friction related to becoming your student.

I am OBSESSED with this. On the order page, I want them to be able to call me 24 hours a day, know exactly what email to send their concerns to, or open a chat directly with my Facebook page. These are all ways I eliminate friction.

You want to make it as easy as possible for your customers to give you money. Losing even ONE sale when someone has come all the way to your order page is a devastating loss that never needs to happen—they simply need to be able to contact you!

There will be specific fears depending on your niche. But there are a few common issues that will hold some people back from taking any course. Here are the most common ones:

- *"I'm not ready, will this work for me…?"*
- *"It's not the right time."*
- *"I don't have time!"*
- *"It's not right for me."*
- *"I'll do it later."*
- *"It's different for me because…"*
- *"I don't even know how to get started…"*
- *"I'm not tech savvy."*
- *"I'm not the kind of person who…"*
- *"What will people think?"*
- *"What if I fail?"*

Consider how you can refute those specific beliefs and how you can replace them with more positive beliefs.

Let's say you're helping people build a professional network. A specific mindset that might hold people back is, "I'm not a people person. I'm an introvert. I'm doomed to be bad at networking." Now, you need to come up with a way to address that objection. How? You could say research shows introverts are better at listening and connecting with people.

Is there a cap on how many students you can handle? Maybe you're offering one-on-one calls or you're reviewing worksheets. If that's the case, let people know there is a limited number of spots available in your course.

How many people need to buy for a $10,000 launch?

HOW MANY SUBSCRIBERS DO YOU NEED TO MAKE $10K?

THE 10K LAUNCH		NO. OF SUBSCRIBERS NEEDED (AT 3% CONVERSION RATE)
UNITS SOLD AT $97	103	~3,433
UNITS SOLD AT $197	50	~1,667
UNITS SOLD AT $497	20	~667
UNITS SOLD AT $997	10	~333
UNITS SOLD AT $1997	5	~167

The $10k launch is a simple way of seeing the numbers laid out in front of you. You can see the right column is the number of subscribers, Facebook group members, email list subscribers, or people interested in what you have to say at a 3% conversion rate, which is reasonable to expect.

You can see you need significantly more traffic to achieve the same launch if you charge lower ticket prices. The sweet spot I've found is $497 and $997, depending on your offer. Never undervalue yourself. What you know is incredibly valuable, and if you care about your students and followers, the money they pay for your guidance is worth it!

Adding daily value and 40 people per day to your Facebook group, YouTube channel, and your email subscribers from your cheatsheet, you can get to 667 followers pretty easily within a few months. If you were consistent for three months, that would mean adding less than eight people per day, which is easily doable!

With 667 followers at a 3% conversion rate with a $997 course, you made $10,000 profit in three months only adding eight people per day!

It's so important to think about this as incremental. Each day you get even ONE new subscriber or follower, you have an INFINITE advantage over your competitors!

Focus on adding value and following the blueprint, and you WILL start to get Facebook group members, email subscribers, and YouTube subscribers!

Launching on YouTube

The most effective way to launch on YouTube is to make a video talking about whatever gets the highest views and most engagement on your channel. If you make ten videos, one of them is going to have more views than the others. Identify that video and make another one on the same topic, because that is the content your audience is interested in. It depends on the topic of your course, but if it's Make Money Online, maybe you get the most views when you make videos on how to make money with SEO.

Most people make the mistake of directly announcing their course, but forget no one cares about you or your course, they only care about themselves!

Make this video, but at the beginning, show off some results, either your own or your students. Announce somewhere in the video you are officially opening your course, but only for the first ten people who want your personal, one-on-one mentorship.

After those ten people join, remove the link from the description below the video. People will naturally wonder if the sale has ended if they watch later, so you want to be really clear for everyone who sees your video!

Launching on Facebook

To launch on Facebook, you want to make a post on your personal Facebook, and more importantly in your Facebook group, showing your students or your own success.

You want to say you are officially opening your Masterclass to ten people, who you will train one-on-one to achieve the same type of success. Once those ten slots are filled, that is it, so they need to act now, or forever hold their peace!

Then, introduce your "Normal'" price. If you intend to sell your product for $997, say your course normally sells for $997, but for the first ten people who sign up, you're going to be taking 50% off today only, and offering the course at the lowest ever price for only $497.

Say that the reason you are doing this is to ensure you have enough capacity to train each and every student one-on-one and give them the attention they need. This establishes scarcity with only ten slots, gives value in the form of your one-on-one attention, and offers them a fast-moving discount, so you hit all the points you need!

You want to end your Facebook post saying, "Comment 'ME' if you want to claim one of the ten spots!" What this does is bump the post so it gets more visibility via engagement in your Facebook group and on your personal FB page!

The reason this happens is when someone comments on a post in your group, it bumps the post to the top of the page, so more people see it! Have your VA tag each person who comments, so they get a push notification to their phone with the direct link to your order page to purchase your course!

I always like to tell people to comment on the post or in the group when they joined as well. This is what I like to call the "Digital Table Rush mentality." When people see other people buying, they get scared they may miss out, so they also join!

You MUST highlight that the opportunity/bonuses/early signup extras are going away and that is happening in the next 12 or 24 hours to create scarcity. People need a reason to take action; otherwise, they won't!

Launching to Your Email List

Your email list will be the smallest of your communication mediums at the beginning, but you want to prepare an email that incites curiosity and drives your followers to join your Facebook group and subscribe to your YouTube channel!

Tell them the same thing as your Facebook post. You want to start with their pain and introduce your vehicle for change to get them to their desire!

You want to show them the success your students are having, and you want to show them how they can have it too. You want to tell them you're opening ten slots, for 50% off, with early sign-up bonuses, that all ends in the next 24 hours!

Step #1: YouTube Launch

Using Amazon as an example, you would want to create a video about Amazon Product Research (because this is the highest traffic subject). At the beginning of the video, tease a special surprise you'll share at the end to make sure they stay, and then at the end, you'll say you're opening your private launch to mentor ten people one-on-one.

Step #2: Facebook Group Launch

You can upload the same video you posted to YouTube directly to your Facebook group. The same day, make a written post announcing that for the next 24 hours only, you are selecting ten people to mentor one-on-one for 50% off of the regular course price. Highlight the benefits of more one-on-one time with you.

Step #3: Email Launch

Craft a few emails driving to your YouTube video launch or Facebook group launch. Incentivize them to join by offering a free cheatsheet, consultation, or something else of value. You always want to give people a reason to do something! You want maximum exposure here because it will be your beast. You also want to give a direct link to the order page as a 'P.S.' at the bottom of your email, something like "Want to fast track your Amazon success? Join my one-on-one mentorship program which opened today—closes in 24 hours!"

Craft two or three emails in total, with curiosity invoking subject lines, like the examples below, again utilizing your most powerful weapons as a marketer! Curiosity, Exclusivity, and Scarcity!

Subject 1: The Best Deal on Earth?

Subject 2: Surprise Inside (Please Open!)

Subject 3: One More Thing…

And that is your launch!

📖 Part 6 Summary

- You learned about the duality between marketing and a good product, and how both are necessary for excellence.
- You learned how to effectively communicate your organic launch using the big three (YouTube, Your Facebook Group, and Your Email List!).
- You learned the importance of mindset and how you must believe it is possible for you, or else you doom yourself by making it impossible.
- You learned how you must believe you deserve it!
- You learned how to frame your story and the importance of your timeline matching your perfect customer.
- You learned about the big three things you MUST have to be successful (being genuine, relatable, and able to invoke emotion!).
- You learned how to properly launch, and how much of a launch happens before you even set out to launch.
- You learned about making your course about one thing, your minimum viable product, and how you need to agitate their pain and future pace.
- You learned how many courses you actually need to sell to achieve the "$10k" launch.
- You learned exactly how to get people to actually take action and join your program, the perfect FB Group launch, YT Launch, and how to do so utilizing curiosity, exclusivity, and scarcity in the right way.

✓ Part 6 Checklist

- Have you determined how you are going to present your story, be genuine, relatable, and match the life timeline of your perfect customers?
- Have you outlined and understood how to launch your course through taking them from their current pain to their desired results?
- Do you understand how to properly use exclusivity and scarcity to incentivize real action from your customers?
- Do you understand the proper way to launch on YouTube, inside Your Facebook Group, and via email?

You are well on your way to creating your empire!

For an in-depth look at 8-Figure marketing strategies, including my best converting ads of all time on Facebook, Google, and YouTube, type www.digitalcoursesecrets.com/go into your web browser now!

Conclusion

Whether it's a split-second decision to talk to a beautiful woman who later becomes your wife and the mother of your children, or a decision to go all in on yourself and stop letting other people dictate your life, sometimes the smallest decisions make the biggest difference in your life.

It's a terrifying idea thinking back to the fateful moment and decision I made sitting in my cubicle, that I was going to go all in on myself.

That one decision created momentum and evolved into a chain reaction that created over $10,000,000 in less than 18 months from nothing, and more importantly changed over 10,000 of my students lives…

Why is it terrifying?

It's a terrifying thought because if I hadn't made that split second decision and commitment to myself, I could STILL be sitting in that cubicle years later, with little or no progress…

So my final advice to you would be stop waiting. There will never be a perfect time to take action. There has never been something like the knowledge economy. It's YOUR TIME!

Dare to take massive action!

Know it will not be perfect. Trust me, your consultation calls are going to feel imperfect, your proof of concept will feel wrong. You're going to doubt the niche you pick.

Most people never want to be in uncomfortable situations. That's what comfort is for them, NEVER feeling uncomfortable. You can reverse these two poles. Make discomfort your new comfort.

When you do that, you are going to be a wild, success-creating machine. You have to be willing to do whatever it takes. This is your time and this is your calling to play a bigger game and become a better person.

Commit to When You Will Finish Your Course!

Choose a completion date for your course and mark it down on your calendar. I want you to get out a calendar right now, look at the dates, and decide you are going to finish your course by a specific date. Maybe it's 60 days from now or 90 days from now, but I want you to get it on your calendar.

All of this hard work will pay off beyond your wildest dreams, and will change your entire life when you do it right. So, put in the work now, and then plan to celebrate when you finish!

The next step is continuing to create beautiful content on YouTube and fostering and growing your Facebook community, helping more and more people achieve their wildest desires!

Humans connect with other humans, and you want to use this to your advantage! You want micro commitments in the form of reading your posts, watching your videos and learning about what you have to offer, looking at testimonials, and seeing what is included in your course!

The more people hear about your offer and see social proof of its validity through testimonials, the more likely they are to buy. Learning and understanding ActiveCampaign and ClickFunnels is insanely valuable to any and every business in the world.

Entrepreneurship is a beautiful process and a journey of non-stop learning, growth, and evolution. By enjoying the process rather than solely focusing on the goal, you can live a happier life than you ever could have imagined. You can create your own empire while helping others and finding fulfillment in the process!

Make sure you join our free Facebook group by heading to Facebook and typing "Digital Course Secrets" into the search bar.

Remember you NOW have an *Unfair Advantage*. You're not satisfied with average and being the pinball in life. You understand it's YOUR time, and if you don't get started building your dreams, someone will hire you to help build theirs!

If you're ready to join an exclusive group filled with millionaire entrepreneurs who ALL started as complete beginners reading this book just like you are right now...

OR

If you're a decisive person and you recognize there has never been an opportunity like the knowledge economy and are ready to get started today, then visit www.digitalcoursesecrets.com/go, *scroll to the bottom,* and join our family right now!

You know the knowledge economy is the next biggest thing, you know people are making this happen every day, and you know the blueprint, now you need a proven mentor to help you one-on-one throughout the entire process!

Join today from our special link and get 50% off the normal course price (to claim the 50% off, visit the below link AND scroll to the bottom of the page!)

Special Link: www.digitalcoursesecrets.com/go

(Visit the link simply by typing it into your normal web browser - and don't forget the /go on the end! It should look like the picture below!)

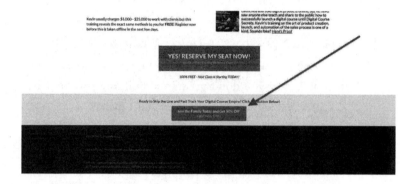

If you already have a successful business and want to scale it to 7 or even 8 figures and beyond, visit
www.TheInfinityMastermind.com
to *schedule your free strategy session* today!

Remember, the choices you make determine where you are in life. If I hadn't made the ONE small decision to become an entrepreneur, you wouldn't be reading this right now.
Take action- let's do this together!

Bonus Chapter

This bonus chapter is the summation of the ten most valuable lessons I've learned going from an anxious, depressed accountant trapped in a cubicle to creating my dream life.

1. The knowledge economy is the next big thing, and anyone who tells you differently is trying to sell you something. It's approaching a billion dollars per DAY business and growing. I've never found something that can compete with building a following and selling a digital product. You can press a button, and $100,000 magically appears in your bank account. It's pretty GREAT, and you can cross promote other people's courses, do affiliate marketing, scale with paid traffic, so on and so forth. The truth is, time passes whether you get better at (for example) buying/selling physical real estate or you get better at selling a digital course on buying/selling real estate, but they're WILDLY different business models with different capital outlays, different levels of manual work, human capital, and infinitely different risk models. There's no other business model I've come across where you can build a $10MM+ business in a little over 1.5 years with only one employee in the US, and I would argue it doesn't exist.

2. Focus on one person you know has done what you want to do and block out all other noise. For me, this was Russell Brunson who,

unknowingly, was a major influence in my life. I've only spoken to him twice. The first time we spoke was on stage when I was getting a 2 Comma Club Award for a million dollars made in one funnel, and I told him I would see him next year for the 8-Figure award. The second time we spoke was when I was getting the 8-Figure award the following year. I remember asking if he was going to make a new award. You can have incredibly impactful mentors even without ever meeting in real life through the power and beauty of the internet!

3. Try to look beyond what successful people are talking about and, instead, focus on what they're DOING with their time. For example, if someone is telling you crypto is the best new way to make money online, and they're selling a course on it, they're actually spending their time selling digital courses, not selling crypto. It's infinitely less risky and has ridiculously high profit margins and potential for scale. Emulate success until you have it with an unstoppable laser focus on what successful entrepreneurs DO with their time, not what they say.

4. Understanding the motivation behind why people and companies say and do what they do is incredibly important to making the best data-driven decisions. Making a few large decisions correctly will completely change your life. The unfortunate truth is that people often have selfish incentives for doing and saying things. If you habituate understanding WHY people are saying and doing things, you'll be capable of making more rational, logical decisions, and you'll drastically increase the likelihood of those decisions being correct. For example, if an entrepreneur you know and follow is recommending a software platform as the best and he owns it, or they have the best affiliate payouts, maybe you should question whether that software is actually best for you and your business, or if it just is best for him!

5. Recognize Shiny Object Syndrome as a toxic addiction and learn to identify and silence it. There will always be some person telling you LinkedIn, Snapchat, or TikTok is the next big thing, and they're making a million dollars a day with it. They're not. Focus makes millionaires, and focus is two-fold. You have to focus on what you should do, and also focus on what you should not do. Stay accountable to yourself on your priorities and block out all noise and distractions.

6. Habits are what differentiate wildly successful people. What is the difference between a billionaire and homeless person? Habits. Habits start with ONE day, so only focus on TODAY. Make small changes, one at a time. You can't go cold turkey on all social media in an instant, completely change your diet, become a bodybuilder overnight, or learn to meditate in a day. It takes time, so stick with it. Albert Einstein said, "Compound interest is the eighth wonder of the world. He who understands it, earns it...he who doesn't...pays it." Small changes add up over time. Trust the process and take things one day at a time, continuously improving.

7. Understand Feedback Cycles: Belief > Actions > Results > Re-Affirm Belief = invincible feedback cycle. If I could go back in time and tell myself ONE thing before I began, I would say, "Start immediately. There's always a million reasons not to; once you do start, never ever stop. You made it because, no matter what anyone ever said to you, you ignored it. I don't care if your parents, your friends, your wife/husband, your co-workers, your teachers, or ANYONE tells you to get a normal job and to play it safe. Respectfully ignore it, respectfully burn the bridges, and go all in on yourself–you will be successful. It's not a question of if; it's just a matter of when. It doesn't matter how high you climb the ladder if

it's leaned against the wrong building. Don't waste your time making someone else rich. You get good at what YOU DO. Time is the universal constant, and it passes whether you're building your empire or someone else's, so get to work."

8. Think for yourself. I didn't have any traditional mentors, so I built my business my own way, and I didn't learn any bad habits. Go against the grain. I didn't work so hard to leave the 9-5 and my cubicle just to go get a big office building again myself, with 100x more responsibility since I would be running the company. Build a virtual empire and hire internationally. Some of my smartest co-workers (I try to never refer to anyone as an employee, since we are all equals) work with me internationally. I've found international friends/co-workers willing to grind sixteen hour days with me when necessary, who are significantly less entitled, and are of the utmost quality and value. Not having a big expensive office and employees allows you to spend more on paid traffic and he who spends the most to acquire a customer wins. Without your team and culture you create, you're nothing. Start a catch phrase and live it everyday #TeamNoExcuses.

9. Understand and relentlessly pursue the low hanging fruit. You can spend your time in a million different ways, some of which add more automation to your life and some of which add less. Often times, additional employees and people are what introduce additional work and stress into your life. You can focus on scaling paid traffic, or you can hire more staff. Oftentimes, both produce the same results (more money), but one requires infinitely less time and energy for the same additional gain. When you decide what to focus your time on, always choose what furthers automation. At the end of the day, whether you're making $10MM a year or $50MM a year, I promise that

you'll be more happy with $10MM if you have what's more important than financial freedom: time freedom. The only difference between a liquid multi-millionaire and a billionaire is a private jet and a yacht. Think long and hard if you want those 2 things. If you do—you need to dedicate your ENTIRE life and every single decision for your whole life to reaching that point. If you're like me and don't need to be a billionaire, be happy and grateful for what you do have, and create temporal freedom (the most important thing of all).

10. Search for the platinum link in your niche. Understand what most people need and what is most profitable for you to provide. For example, when I was deciding what to make my Amazon software on, I could have chosen to make inventory forecast software or profitability software, which only a small percentage the largest sellers need, or I could have chosen to make a software on product research and keywords, which all beginners need. Same market, same situation, wildly different ceiling for scale. You can start the next Facebook or Uhaul, both profitable companies, but very different models. Another example is an airline. Expedia makes more from the sale of a ticket than the airport or airlines, even though Expedia does SO MUCH LESS WORK than the airlines. The airlines have employees, depreciation of assets, physical planes, and buildings, but make less money; why? Being rich in the not-so-distant past equated to owning the most stuff, farms, land, etc. Now, being rich equates to owning the most attention. Attention is literally a currency and arguably the most POWERFUL one—that is why building a personal brand and adding real value/caring about your followers is the most valuable thing you can do!

I hope you've enjoyed this book as much as I enjoyed writing it. It's a strange thing, writing a book, compacting years of blood, sweat, and tears into a few pages.

I know that most people will read this book and think, "Huh, some pretty good ideas in there," and that will be the end of it.

Others will get a huge rush of motivation which will fizzle a day or a week or a month later without much results.

And then there is you.

The beautiful thing about being a human being is that you have the power of free will.

With just the information contained inside this small book, you can choose to change your entire life. You can choose to change your family's life. You can choose to change everything and write your own history.

But it's up to you to be relentless, laser focused, and implement consistently like there's no tomorrow.

If you're ready to take control of your life and of YOUR unfair advantage today, learn more for free at www.DigitalCourseSecrets.com/go

Or, if you want one-on-one help from me personally and already have a successful business looking to scale, visit www.TheInfinityMastermind.com now!

Because remember: failure doesn't exist, only feedback.

Your friend,
Kevin David

About the Author

KEVIN DAVID is the CEO and founder of THATLifestyleNinja and has been featured in Forbes, Entrepreneur, The Wall Street Journal, and INC. He graduated Summa Cum Laude with a double major in Accountancy and Business Information Systems. Kevin worked at the prestigious accounting firm  PriceWaterhoueCoopers and then as a consultant at Facebook but ultimately realized that he was not destined to work for anyone else. In a very short period of time after leaving the 9-5 world, he successfully launched his own Amazon FBA business and proceeded to teach others how to follow in his footsteps, leaving the corporate grind behind.

Kevin was the fastest ever to achieve the "2 Comma Club" award, offered by popular software startup Clickfunnels, which signifies entrepreneurs earning 1 million dollars from a single sales funnel. In February of 2019, he received a prestigious "2 Comma Club X," an award given to entrepreneurs who earn over $10,000,000 from a sales funnel.

Today, Kevin is recognized as a global expert and trainer in building profitable, viral online businesses. Kevin's work is mainly notable for the creation of his digital courses, his YouTube presence, and large Facebook communities. His videos on Youtube have over 15 million views, and he has over six hundred thousand subscribers. He has built a robust community with over a million people in his various programs and social media following.